For Mary
To our past
May one glance at you
continue to bring out the best in
me
Carrying me like a majic carpet
that is following the thread,
With Love,
Peter

THE MONOGAMY CHALLENGE

Creating and Keeping Intimacy

By Peter Kane

The Monogamy Challenge
Published through Relationship Transformations Press

Interior Book Design and Cover by
www.integrativeink.com

ISBN 978-0-9843596-0-8

For more information contact:
www.peterkane.org

To my mother, for teaching me how to be a man in the way that she faced the challenges of being a woman.

To my father, for caring and giving me a childhood without the abuse he endured.

To my kids, for their emotional intelligence and for inspiring me and teaching me to be as a child again.

CONTENTS

ACKNOWLEDGMENTS

This book represents much of my life's work, so every person and every aspect of my life has supported me in writing this. My entire career has been filled with students and clients who have taught me about their lives. I have had peers and teachers who have supported my learning and personal healing. I have had friends and partners that have supported, inspired, stretched, loved, empowered, seasoned, softened, and taught me as well. I will do my best to name a few of these.

Most of my career, I have had more peers than teachers. This is one disadvantage of being a teacher who is exploring newer relationship technologies. I would, however, like to thank Leonard Orr, who was one of my early teachers. I thank Leonard for being a leader in creating breathwork as we know it today. It is also my feeling that Leonard actually broke ground toward many of the more advanced relationship models of our time. I would also like to thank the many peers that helped me to continue with breathwork and relationship training: Sondra Ray, Bill Chappelle, Bob and Mallie Mandel, Fred Lehrman, Phil Laut, Jim Morningstar, and Diane Hinterman, to name a few.

In the more recent years, as I wrote this manuscript, I have only cited two teachers whom I currently acknowledge as teachers. They are Hal and Sidra Stone. Their work with The Psychology of Selves and the Voice Dialogue Process are two of the models I use in this book; but more importantly, my relatively brief times as their student have given me a much-needed feeling of support and the knowledge that I was not alone in my efforts.

I would like to thank the many organizers, producers, and assistants who have hosted seminars, workshops, and trainings, which I have facilitated over the years. It is a beautiful thing to have people trust me enough to produce my workshops.

I am very grateful for the Esalen Institute and all the people who were there when I was a work scholar at Esalen in 1978. The people and processes there helped me heal as I was grieving the loss of my father, and they also provided exceptional training and vision as I began my education as a counselor.

I thank the faculty and students at Antioch University, Seattle. My experience as a student there in 1994 and 1995 did more for me, and my writing, than I would have ever imagined. Thank-you Candace, Cynthia, Dan, Randy, and Sue, to name a few.

I am particularly grateful to Betty Estelle, who has been a dear friend and teacher since we met at Esalen in 1978. It was Betty who encouraged me to pursue breathwork and a career in counseling, and her powerful guidance was instrumental in trusting my career path and myself.

I would like to thank some of the many friends who have supported me in writing and the writing and editing of this manuscript: Bill, Camilla, Carol, Cathy, Darla, Joy, Kathy,

Acknowledgments

Kelly, LeAnn, Len, Max, Rob, and Sarah. I thank Loreen for helping create a beautiful cover. My deepest thanks also go to my sister for her consistent encouragement.

I am very grateful to Stephanee Killen at Integrative Ink for her wonderful edits and support with the publishing process.

And thank you to my stepmother, who taught me, when I was fourteen, that there was more to life and relationships than met the eye, and for opening my eyes to the existence of metaphysical literature, spirituality, alternative therapies, and personal growth.

INTRODUCTION

We use strong words to describe sexual infidelity: adultery, betrayal, and cheating, just to name a few. At some level, we accept that monogamy is difficult for many men and women. We also expect people to be monogamous if they want to have a successful relationship. However, we were not taught how to be monogamous. We are not given training on how to navigate the myriad of desires that might compel us to have sex with someone other than our partner. We are surrounded by conservative assumptions that monogamy is easy on one hand, and a thriving sex and pornography industry on the other.

Most of us have probably learned that it hurts our partner to hear about our attractions to others. Our partner's fantasies hurt us, and it devastates us if they have sex with others or leave us for a new lover. Our culture is saturated with sexual tension and the challenge of how to have a monogamous relationship. We don't talk about it because we would prefer to see it as our neighbor's problem. We wouldn't want our partner to feel threatened or think that we are one of those weak people who may go astray. We may also prefer to keep up appearances and insure that the world views us as a "happy couple." We have had little help in identifying and resolving the challenges we face.

On top of this, the sexual vitality of a relationship tends to wane once the "honeymoon" is over. This stagnation combined with the tendency to be attracted to others drives people to move on to new partners and lose the richness that long-term relationships provide. If we suppress our sexuality or our attractions to others, it just adds to the problem by dampening our current sexual connection.

There are solutions that include several aspects of relationships. We need tools for creating strong, intimate relationships; we need to learn how to maintain intimacy in current relationships; and we need support for dealing with non-monogamous feelings. This book is about all of this. It is about how to sustain and deepen intimacy and work through non-monogamous feelings. It is about understanding attractions, learning from them, and creating a new context where attractions can be a source of personal growth. My purpose is to help you resolve what fuels your attractions. The book also includes deep relationship work that will support any relationship need or goal.

Accepting Sexual Attractions

Dictionaries define monogamy as being married to one person at a time. I am using the term to address sexual partnership and define monogamy as having one lover. It is also important to note that I am not necessarily criticizing people for having more than one lover if that is their choice, unless they profess to be monogamous but are not. In all cases, my goal is to increase our understanding of what drives us to be monogamous or not and how to continue to grow toward ever increasing intimacy in our relationships.

My focus will be slanted only slightly more toward the challenges that monogamous men face, partly because I am a man, and partly because the common perception is that men have greater difficulty maintaining monogamous relationships. If we could remove the pain that adultery has caused from our history, we would live in a much-improved world. If we could address the challenges involved in creating and sustaining monogamous relationships, many of us would be much happier. It is fair to say that men have affairs more often than women, although our sexual issues and patterns have resulted in affairs by both genders. It is also helpful to address the issues beyond their connection to gender because sometimes it is a woman who is more attracted to others, is having affairs, or wants a deeper sexual connection than her partnership currently has. In particular, I will address some male dilemmas as well as monogamy challenges from a gender-neutral perspective. This book is also about how to sustain a monogamous relationship when your partner desires less sex than you do.

I believe that monogamy has deep spiritual and psychological value, and that creating a vital monogamous relationship can be challenging. I have been in monogamous relationships for most of my life, including a marriage of sixteen years. I will share some of the challenges I have faced over these years. As my friend and teacher Hal Stone put it, "Monogamy is painful." Hal is the only person I have ever met who was more honest about monogamy and his erotic attractions to other women than I was, and since hearing his honesty, I have become more honest myself.

I include parts of my story as relevant case studies or chronicles. I believe the teacher or researcher does not sit outside of his or her topic, and a study is more objective when we know the position of the teacher or reporter. When a teacher's position is explicit, we are better able to consider our own feelings. If teachers don't speak about themselves, it implies that they have completely mastered their topic. If a teacher shares their own struggle with the information, it helps students become more accepting of themselves and go into greater depth.

When I use examples of clients or students, I have changed their names and omitted any details that would reveal their identity. I will be honest in the telling of relevant parts of my history, and I have also changed the names and some of the details of the other participants. I hope my honesty helps you connect more deeply with how this material can apply to you, and that you will be encouraged to explore your own chronicles.

There may be those who assert that this book is unnecessary because monogamy is easy. If monogamy is easy for you, I congratulate you, but I suggest the possibility that the lack of conflict does not necessarily mean real peace. Often it means extreme dissociation from something that is too uncomfortable to deal with. My intent is to bring taboo sexual feelings of non-monogamy out into the open so that they can be accepted and put into a perspective that allows us to have them and remain monogamous. It will be easier to understand parts of this book if you can already relate to the issue of having non-monogamous feelings.

I explore some of the virtues of monogamy and difficulties monogamous couples face, in addition to many of the anthropological, cultural, and sexual issues that intersect and make up the anatomy of monogamy. The last sections of the book, Facing the Challenge and Additional Resources, will include a variety of tools that you can use to support yourself in maintaining a monogamous relationship.

If you're not sure whether this topic is relevant to you, I can simplify it by offering two categories into which most monogamous people could fit: those who accomplish monogamy by cutting off their erotic/romantic feelings or (their) connections to other people, and those who deal with the difficult issues of having erotic/romantic feelings toward people other than their partner. For example, I have never really bonded unconditionally with a female friend without also having the awareness of her as a sexual being with whom it would be enjoyable to make love. Noticing this aspect of my connection and not "freaking out" about it is essential to my remaining a friend in the fullest sense of the word. If I were to avoid my sexual feelings, I would enter a state of distance or withdrawal. I have seen monogamous people judge, dislike, or even quarrel with friends and associates as a means of remaining at a safe distance sexually. This is much the same dynamic as when some fathers fight with their daughters, particularly in puberty, in order to keep their sexual attraction repressed and maintain safe boundaries. Mothers do this, too, but this behavior appears to be more common with fathers.

Avoiding our attractions creates stagnation, and intimacy wanes as resentments build. It may happen that attractions to certain types of people keep occurring. I do not suggest that we act on our attractions in order to "get them out of our system." Both denying our attractions or acting on them have the likelihood of weakening or destroying our relationship with our partner. Instead, I am presenting a third option: when we learn what drives attractions, we learn things about ourselves and our needs that can potentially deepen our relationship with our partner. Attractions can be viewed, accepted, and even appreciated as a gift, which when opened and looked at, can reveal to us qualities that are needed but have been missing from our monogamous relationship. Working on developing those qualities together can deepen the intimacy and joy that we experience with our partner. In the process, the object of the attraction becomes less important because the attraction is no longer driven by the feelings of lack in our relationship.

These concepts also apply to same-sex relationships, and I intend to write without heterosexism or homophobia. You may notice my use of unique pronouns or vocabulary, and I will not assume that a marriage is between a man and a woman. To me, a marriage is any emotionally committed relationship whether legally recognized by the state or not. Also, to give an even subtler example, when I write about a child's guardian or parent(s), I do not assume that the child has a father or a mother in a traditional sense. A child may be in foster care. A child's parents can be any combination of committed men or women. A father can be absent or even just a sperm donor. A child can have one, two, or more mothers. Or its mother may be a biological surrogate only and a child may have one or more fathers. I feel it is very important for heterosexuals to get comfortable with this kind of vocabulary and take themselves out of being "the norm" or "the only," just as we do when we take white men out of "the center" when we stop assuming that all Medical Doctors are white men.

The focus here is on relationships and more specifically sexual desire in relationships. There is nothing wrong with a man or woman having more testosterone or sex drive than their partner. In fact, based on the principles of how we are attracted to someone who has energies that are opposite ours, we are likely to enter long-term relationships with someone with a greater or lesser sex drive than our own. The anthropological and social perspective that men are often more sexually motivated than women is part of this book, but this is also an unfair generalization. I will discuss relationships where one individual, regardless of gender, is more sexually interested than the other. I will offer insight and tools about how couples (and singles) can create balance in their sexual desires and sustain monogamy regardless of the nature of their sexual feelings.

All feelings are innocent in nature, and sexual feelings are normal. My goal is to help you, the reader, release subconscious sexual shame and help you identify whether you feel, on some level, as if you should apologize for being sexual. This is an important step for all of us. It is completely innocent to be sexual, and here we will explore the differences between this innocence and our behavior. The more innocent we feel, the less likely we will behave in ways that cause others pain. Feeling innocent about our sexuality is also a key aspect of our feeling worthy of love in general, and worthiness helps us attract a committed and monogamous partner.

We have all had numerous forces that have suppressed our essential nature as sexual and physical beings. This book pushes against our history of sexual suppression and repression. It is an exploration of embracing sexual innocence while maintaining monogamous relationships, and it will offer insights on how best to do both. Whatever your relationship to your sexuality, I hope to support you in creating a deeper connection with your sexual innocence.

This book is about more than sexuality and monogamy. Many couples will notice that, as they work with sex and intimacy issues, the same dynamic occurs in other areas, like communication and finances. This is because sexuality issues are governed by core patterns or relationship dynamics. A couple's basic issues will affect virtually every area of the relationship. Sex and monogamy are deep and important issues to explore, and addressing them will also help address other relationship patterns.

❧ PART I ☙
THE VIRTUES OF MONOGAMY

CHAPTER 1
WHY PREFER MONOGAMY?

Before I state the case for monogamy and some of the deeper reasons I feel people value monogamy, I want to note that it is helpful to view the desire for monogamous relationships as a subjective preference. The ideas I'm sharing stem from the assumption that readers want monogamous relationships, although this is just one of many possible priorities in relationships. It is best to view monogamy as a personal preference and not as an issue to be categorized as right or wrong. Like any choice in life, we are entitled to what we want, and no explanation is needed.

It is, however, helpful if we realize what makes monogamy preferable for us. Understanding what drives our preferences will make it easier for us to feel strong and clear about deserving them and will help us focus on accomplishing them. Being specific about why we need monogamy will help us communicate with a potential partner. Just asking for monogamy itself is almost too general and can also bring up notions of right and wrong. For example, it would work better if we explain to someone that we prefer a certain feeling of emotional safety and that for us, monogamy is a necessary part of that. Being more specific takes the conversation away from the value judgments people tend to attach to monogamy and brings the conversation down to real issues.

Monogamy is a practical part of what many people need to feel safe enough to love deeply. Like it or not, most of us tend to hold back if we feel that someone might leave us. If our lover has another lover, we may feel insecure and not go as deeply into intimacy. This is another way of saying that we prefer the security that comes with monogamy and permanent relationships.

This can also be effectively described with regard to an aspect of ourselves commonly referred to as our inner-child. Just as we grow up and develop strong adult aspects, we also have vulnerable child aspects. We are not one-dimensional beings; we have many different feelings and issues within us. Old vulnerable feelings from our infancy and childhood still exist and live within us. Understanding this and the impact these feelings have on relationships is essential if we are to address relationship issues effectively. Our vulnerable child can be the driving force behind issues of sadness and fear, as well as our seemingly more adult behaviors. Often, our adult ways of being exist as a means of protecting our vulnerable inner child. A classic example is defensiveness. While it can look like a rational adult behavior, the driving force behind it is often a scared, vulnerable child.

In the area of sexuality and monogamy, it is helpful if we understand that our vulnerable inner child needs security and stability. It does not want to be left and is therefore likely to prefer monogamy. It is also helpful to realize that our inner child does not care about, or enjoy sex. It likes the closeness and security that comes from close affection, but sex itself is beyond its interest. The vulnerable child does love intimacy. Part of the softness, richness, and deep love that is included in intimacy involves our feeling that our vulnerable inner-child is being seen, cared for, and nourished.

Being in contact with our inner-child does not mean that we have created a parent substitute to take care of us. The vulnerable inner-child can be included in a healthy adult relationship if both individuals are connected to and supporting their own inner-child and sharing this aspect with the other. It will also make for a healthier relationship if both people support the other's inner-child to a similar degree. Having a strong connection with our inner-child can increase the depth of love because its vulnerability brings out a deeper, more resonant and present love. If the vulnerable side of love is present along with the more powerful adult side, then that vulnerability actually creates a balance that takes intimacy deeper. If both partners are giving and receiving nurturing somewhat equally, the relationship will become more balanced, not less.

Social order is another category within which our preference for monogamy can be explained. Here the desire for monogamy is because it enables people to fit into the way our society is organized around couples, families, and nuclear families. There are many reasons I would encourage people to resist fitting into contemporary culture, especially as many of our family practices and traditions are unhealthy. But, in the end, I would suggest that monogamy is important enough to most people that we accept the need for it. Monogamy is a far-reaching component of our social structure, and it is somewhat inevitable that most of us will feel more comfortable in monogamous relationships—our culture just doesn't offer support for open or non-monogamous relationships.

It is interesting to entertain the possibility that the issue of social order is of equal or greater influence than the security, jealousy, or vulnerable child issues. Although it is possible that vulnerability and abandonment issues are the primary reasons most people don't want open relationships, another major reason is that there is not much support within the larger system for it. If we were surrounded by open or group marriages, we might be part of a community that supported each other in working through vulnerability issues. We would also have more partners to help us remain aware of our non-monogamous side. And, if we had a primary partner who was out with another person, instead of being home alone feeling anxious about it, we would be out with another partner.

It is valuable to strive to transcend cultural norms and not just do something because it is what others do. On the other hand, we have a human need to belong and be connected to our culture. The phrase to *be in the world but not of it* expresses this well. I like to be connected to the world but not a habitual follower of cultural norms. For example, I might attend a neighborhood party but not necessarily drink or eat the same things as everyone else. My children might go to public school, but I may nurture or discipline them according to my own standards and not by assumed cultural standards. In the area of monogamy, this would mean I might live in a community where the majority of couples are monogamous, but I might choose to have multiple lovers. Yet, in the area of marriage and monogamy, the hurdles may be too large to do this. To deal with the vulnerability of open relationships, my emotional body would need more support than is currently offered by most of our cultures. I can't help but admire the similar challenge that same sex couples are navigating today, as they become parents together. While different from monogamy issues, same sex couples who raise children are making the deepest stretch in cultural norms in our society today.

Safe sex is another basic need many people have in their desire for monogamy. Here, monogamy is simply practical. This is also a simple topic and a good time to remember that anything you want is okay and acceptable. There is no reason for you to feel guilty or insecure in asking for any preference, especially one that involves your safety. It's easy to practice safe sex until all questions of monogamy, health, and previous sexual history are resolved.

It is important to separate the need for safe sex from the need for an emotionally secure relationship. People often worry about sex from a disease perspective when what is really driving their concerns is the vulnerable inner child's need for security. For example, I have seen people without a prospective date use the fear of disease as a reason to avoid dating. I don't think that single people should overly concern themselves with disease until they are dating someone and considering sex. Once you become sexual, you can use condoms and practice safer sex until all doubt is resolved.

Another reason I encourage monogamy is so you don't feel like a hypocrite. Since you probably don't want your partner sharing their body with another in sexually intimate ways, it is better integrity to give that same security to your partner. Being consistent requires that we resolve our selfishness and be emotionally present and empathetic toward our partner. Holding their needs as equal to our own helps us stay on a path of developing intimacy. Congruency is part of equality, and equality is part of intimacy.

Ideally, we want monogamy because we don't have desire for anyone else. The previous ideas could leave you feeling that monogamy often comes from some duty-bound or insecure place. Monogamy feels best when it is a choice based on the vitality of a relationship, and that vitality results in our not having strong desire for others. While this is the ideal, it is also important to understand that we are all different. Men, for example, may need this book more than women. Some women may need this book more than some men. Some people will use this book to let go of unwanted attractions to people other than their partner. Some people will use it primarily to enhance an existing relationship, and others will use it to create a relationship. Men may need to work with all the issues in this book more rigorously in order to keep their attractions to others in perspective. Each individual's unique challenges do not necessarily diminish their love and devotion to their partner. On some level, all of us who are monogamous can feel that monogamy is an act of love that is natural.

CHAPTER 2
THE SPIRITUAL DEPTH OF MONOGAMY

The idea that monogamy helps a couple reach greater spiritual depth and union is quite common. The deepest purpose of monogamy is not the basic security or cultural issues I have mentioned. Monogamy is a vehicle for creating deep spiritual connection, and it supports sacredness and depth in ways that open relationships do not.

While this perspective may sound religious or traditional, what I am trying to share here is validated by the most contemporary views of relationships. Spiritual depth is an energetic issue that goes beyond religious beliefs and encompasses the psychological, mental, and physical realms. Doing deep work on the psychological and physical levels creates a foundation for the spiritual level. Without the psychological and physical issues addressed, spiritual ideals are superficial because they are covering up other drives. The real depth that monogamy offers is only accessible when the emotional and psychological issues are addressed.

The simplest point in favor of monogamy is that monogamy creates a connection and trust that takes a relationship deeper. Sometimes the depth of a partnership creates deep joy and just makes us feel monogamous. As the partnership grows, monogamy creates oneness and a context for continual deepening. While we might experience this deepening as primarily connected to our vulnerable child's opening and trusting, this can also be explained in spiritual terms. Oneness and security are not just remedies for loss or insecurity. They are spiritual states. In the area of sexuality, most people feel monogamy is the best vehicle for oneness. As a couple continues to be monogamous over time, they continually build increasing levels of trust, connection, and intimacy.

This deepening is potentially difficult to feel because as relationships grow, so too do conflicts and negative patterns. But it is not monogamy's fault that committed monogamous relationships can tend to challenge us or stagnate. There are many personal issues that are not even sexual in nature, which negatively impact relationships. If we separate the virtues of monogamy from other relationship problems, we have a better chance of creating vital monogamous relationships. Monogamy holds an essence of its own that is of deep spiritual value, which will be more easily enjoyed if we actively seek to resolve the other issues that come up in relationships.

The spiritual value of monogamy can also be articulated by viewing how non-monogamous relationships are often felt to be superficial or lacking in intimacy. In non-monogamous situations, people tend to spend energy making sure that partners don't find out much about their other relationships. My favorite definition of intimacy is *in-to-me-see*. Closeness comes from being seen and allowing people to see you. You can't do this if you have secrets or topics you prefer to avoid. Even if it is only a few topics that are being avoided, the energy spent making sure you *do not* talk about sensitive issues will affect other areas. The best way to be completely intimate is to remain completely open and without secrets or taboo topics.

Another way to highlight how monogamous relationships are more intimate is to notice that if someone is secretly non-monogamous, all parties involved know it on some level. People always know the truth; they just don't know that they know it. Their conscious mind might not recognize it, but their gut instincts will. If someone discovers their partner is having an affair, they are usually not surprised. This illustrates that the affair was negatively affecting the depth of the relationship on many levels. Conversely, this describes how monogamy creates much positive energy, such as trust, certainty, and safety. If you're monogamous, your partner will be more relaxed and secure. Security is not just a mundane physical quality; it is the physical basis for moving in a forward direction spiritually. Spiritual security is the basis for expanding into increased joy and aliveness. It is the basis of ecstasy.

The truth might just be that if we are seeking oneness, the only way to be "one" is to be "one." Perhaps no matter how hard we try, if we are with others there will be part of our spiritual essence that will hold back. True spiritual union results in a desire to give ourselves fully to our partner. While saying, "give ourselves to our partner" does create a potential problem with possession and stagnation issues I'll be addressing later, if we adjust this language to "share myself fully with my partner" then we have the ability to receive the depth of monogamy without the potential limitations.

The basic argument has always been that the more you can share yourself fully, the deeper the intimacy. There are those who feel that they can share themselves fully without monogamy, but personally, I can go deeper emotionally, psychologically, and spiritually if I am monogamous. I feel that oneness is a spiritual quality or essence, and that the personal sexual form of oneness is more easily created within monogamous relationships.

❦ PART II ❧
THE ARCHETYPES OF MARRIAGE
AND MONOGAMY

CHAPTER 3
THE OLD ARCHETYPE OF MARRIAGE AND MONOGAMY

The archetype of marriage is the cultural and personal expectations that we attach to marriage, most of which are subconscious. Understanding our unconscious negative expectations and archetypes of marriage offers an explanation of some marriage problems. No matter how hard you work to avoid replaying negative personal or social marriage patterns, the act of entering into a marriage contract brings energies and meanings into the relationship, which go beyond the individuals themselves. A marriage contract could be seen as having its own subconscious meanings, and the act of marriage adds those meanings to the relationship regardless of the other essential qualities of the relationship.

This chapter is valuable for everyone because the old archetype of marriage and monogamy affects all forms of committed relationships. The closer the commitment comes to marriage, the more it affects a relationship. For example, the archetype probably surfaces the most when two people live together. As I proceed, I will be referring to this as a marriage issue, but I mean to include all forms of commitment. If you are not married or do not intend to seek marriage, you can replace the term marriage with monogamy or commitment.

The archetype of marriage can be divided into personal, cultural, and universal origins. Within the personal realm are the issues that come from our own history and attitudes. Here, terms like family patterns, family tradition, abandonment, suffocation, neediness, and traditional marriages begin to express the many issues we can bring to our own personal archetype of marriage. The term cultural archetype helps us note that many of our issues originate from beyond our immediate personal or family experience and are inherited from society as a whole. There is a strong connection between the personal and cultural because in order for the culture to impact us, we have to agree with it personally on some level. The term cultural archetype expresses how some of the issues come from a broader experience, beyond our own personality or history; they come from society at large.

Our histories with our family and society have given us expectations, and we bring them with us into our marriage contracts. For example, you could say that the purpose of this book is to transcend the archetype that says marriage results in a lack of sexual connection. Some people even have the belief or archetype that married people are often not monogamous. This is, in a sense, an archetype in which an individual gets married and enters into the subconscious expectation that his or her partner may have an affair.

There are many archetypes based on gender roles where marriage means that a certain person handles money, or a kind of domestic chore. There are communication archetypes that would result in non-communication or the belief that married men are less communicative than married women. There are emotional archetypes where one person is allowed to communicate anger and the other isn't. There are religious archetypes that view one gender as superior or closer to a higher power.

In my work, I have usually referred to these archetypes as "patterns" or as "telepathic agreements." We get married and fall into subconscious expectations or agreements to be a certain way. Here the term archetype helps to connect this notion to the possibility that there may also be some universal characteristics of marriage and of emotionally committed relationships that will inevitably be added to relationships we seek to be permanent. These would include both expansive and contractive characteristics. By expansive, I mean that it may be inevitable that when we commit to a permanent relationship, we tap into a universal energy of increased devotion that will deepen the relationship. This is one way to describe what many people who marry may be seeking. By contractive, I mean that when we seek a permanent relationship, we may also be acting on principles of control and possession. We may not simply be committing but are also seeking a safe haven from our fears, which would eventually manifest regardless of the strength of the relationship.

The old archetype of marriage is possession, and not love or commitment. By getting married, we may be buying into issues that go beyond cultural expectations and programming and into universal principles of relationship. Consciously or not, a major intent of those who become legally married is to create security. Thus, they buy into and are affected by security and possession issues that take them away from the unconditional and deeper experience of heartfelt commitment. Simply put, some of us get married to ensure that we will always have a source of love and that we will not be abandoned. This drive for security can create a quality of possessiveness, which stifles the aliveness of a relationship.

The motivation to possess a permanent relationship actually results in the manifestation of our fears. The controlling nature of possession both stifles relationships and burdens them with the fears of loss from which people were originally seeking relief. By holding on to our partner, we validate and perpetuate the fear of loss that a permanent relationship may have been designed to solve in the first place. When we try to possess someone, it will accentuate any tendency they have to run away from intimacy. Both people are also likely to feel an increased suppression that comes with feeling possessed like an object.

Relationships work best when we learn to surrender control and trust. If we approach marriage from a control or security perspective, we are bringing a contractive energy to our relationships—the old archetype of marriage based on ownership rather than commitment. Think back—a century ago, married women were essentially the property of their husbands. The drive for stability and security is similar to that of ownership. These problems were very real in our not too distant past, and we are still recovering from them. Feminism has alerted us to this, but the same is true for men. Being a husband is a false and stifling identity, just as being a wife is. Many married men complain of feeling like a pack animal or a "beast of burden." The definition of the word husband is laden with possessive terms like "householder" and "to dwell." These imply male superiority and an increased sense of burden that leave many men feeling as if their worth comes from what they possess and not from their emotional or spiritual nature.

The act of joining into a deep relationship involves being committed, but also free of the negative archetypes of possession that can come with commitment. The key is to find and express our love and commitment from a free place. Commitment can be a free experience that comes from our heart, from real love, and from joy. Too often commitment has come from a duty bound or obligated place that stifles relationships.

Another key word that expresses what commitment means is presence. To be present is to *be with,* and being with our partner creates more oneness with them on an energetic level. By committing to and being present with others, we also become more present on this earth. By being present, our rewards increase because we have more power to attract things when we are present. Many of the negatives in life can be seen clearly if we notice the component of not being present. By being emotionally numb and withdrawn, both our physical health and relationships suffer. By being here, our vitality increases. By committing to our lives, partners, and children, we become present with ourselves on a deeper level.

Commitment is a key to freedom. Presence and commitment create freedom because when you are fully present, you have the ability to expand. Trying to be free is an aspect of avoidance and results in being less present. Often, when we are trying to be free, our investment in being free actually traps us and creates less freedom. We may feel we are moving toward freedom, but our avoidance of relationships creates a state of hovering in suspended animation. If we instead commit to being present here, we have greater ability to move and be free. It is actually by being fully in one place that we are free to move in any direction. Freedom comes from the presence of being here, and we can't be present if we are trying to get away or be free of relationship constraints.

People who are truly committed experience the rewards of their increased presence. Even if they are having problems, if they choose to be present they will find rewards and freedom within their relationship and lifestyle. Commitment and devotion are important and are essential qualities of life. Their importance needs to be balanced with an awareness of the negative archetypes of marriage, but marriage and emotionally committed relationships do include the positive archetypes of commitment and devotion.

For many years, I regularly had conversations with people attending my seminars who were at least partly anti-marriage. They would express ideas similar to those above about marriage being control and possession based, and I would defend my pro-marriage position by defining their position as "commitment phobic," feeling that they lacked the commitment and presence of this earth to devote themselves completely to another. I felt that they were coming from fear of disappointing their beloved, so they kept themselves distant by avoiding marriage. I concluded that they tended to lack the strength to commit to another because they would be unable to handle it if they lost them, thus they never got started.

I have recently revisited these variables in the work of David Schnarch, who addresses them within the rubric of "the strength to want." It takes self-esteem and strength to allow yourself to commit to another because once you're deeply connected, it could be very painful to lose your partner to separation, divorce, or death. Since it takes strength to deal with loss, it takes strength to want, begin, or have a relationship. I consider the process of becoming more present in life and relationships, and having the strength to want, to be a lifetime process that is supported by virtually all therapeutic processes and ideals. I consider much of what I address in this book to be directed toward the goal of becoming more present.

I value marriage and consider myself to be pro-marriage, but I have also come to understand the cynicism so many people have shared with me over the years. The resolution of this is to seek an ongoing emotionally committed relationship that is free of the possessive archetype. To do so will be to create a new archetype of marriage—one that holds committed ideals but also encourages a release and healing of possession and fear patterns.

Chapter 4

The New Archetype of Marriage: Partnership

I believe that the term partnership offers an initial context to create emotionally committed relationships that go beyond the possessive archetype and into a more heart-centered sharing of life. The term partnership communicates equality and can hold devotion without creating the hierarchy that exists between the more traditional husband and wife. Replacing the terms *husband* or *wife* with "partner," and *marriage* with "partnership," enables us to begin a long-term emotionally committed relationship in a context that will more easily allow us to work through the old archetypes of marriage.

I first used the term partner in the late 1970s to create less distinction between couples who were married or monogamous and those who weren't. The meaning of the term grew deeper for me in the '80s when I noticed that same sex couples used it, in part because most states and countries don't allow them the legal benefits of marriage contracts. The term held even more meaning as I began to understand the old archetype of marriage. Both feminism and cultural studies schools of thought often use the term partner because it communicates equality. The terms husband and wife carry a historical taint of hierarchy and inequality, and they also subjugate same sex couples.

Lastly, marriage is often used subconsciously to increase one's social status. By "coming out," or defining ourselves as married, we separate ourselves from the people around us who are not married. Wedding rings are circles that symbolize commitment, but they have also become status symbols. There is nothing wrong with communicating the joy and abundance you feel about your marriage, but doing so also has other effects that are valuable. For this reason, I—and many feminist and cultural studies educators—would recommend that married couples be conscious of their purpose in wearing wedding rings, and use caution in the wearing of those rings if the intent is to communicate wealth and status in addition to commitment. Many relationships also have dependency issues, where they lean on each other and too readily rely on their identity as a couple as a source of security. Since relationships work best when we stand on our own two feet and sooth our own issues from within (as well as get our needs met from our partner), it can be helpful to have our identity as an individual be our primary way of connecting to others. For these reasons, I think that some couples may receive value from having periods where they do not wear wedding rings or wedding rings that communicate wealth.

It is interesting to be heterosexual and use the term partner. Often it makes people wonder if you are homosexual. While addressing this, or the meaning of wedding rings, is not central to the development of the new archetype of marriage, it is a concern that you may need to address. Both feminism and cultural studies encourage members of the dominant culture (married, white, prosperous, and heterosexual) to risk being seen as minorities. If real social change is to occur, members of the dominant class need to risk being seen as homosexual, single, and of modest financial means. So often the opposite is true. We "come out" as married or prosperous by quickly displaying our rings or by talking about a recent vacation. These things can occur in the first few minutes of meeting someone without our realizing that we may have separated ourselves from them by defining our status as different, thus reducing the chances of creating friendship. It is also valuable to clarify that the dominant culture is not the majority. For example, the majority of people are of modest financial means. It is interesting to realize that there is a dominant or controlling culture that is leading us to feel that we should be prosperous, white, heterosexual, and married in order to be good enough.

Conversely, it is worth noting that wedding rings can also create clear and safe boundaries with sexuality and friendship. People are less likely to misinterpret our friendly gestures as flirting if we are wearing a wedding ring. Some people who are single even wear them because they are tired of being approached for sexual reasons. Personally, I feel that Americans are too hung up about this. Another option is to use words to define our status as a conversation or friendship develops instead of displaying a sign or a ring. This can help us feel like individuals instead of possessions. I think this is easier for men because they are less threatened by unwanted sexual advances than women are. Many women are tired of being approached for sexual reasons. If men addressed their more predatory nature, it would be easier to have a society with less distinction between those who are in partnerships and those who are not.

Moving back to some of the deeper issues, the term partner not only communicates a sense of equality but it also communicates that partnerships can be ended. This is a healthy thing, which is not contrary to commitment, because a commitment should be re-thought if it becomes unhealthy. Partnership is an equal term that communicates that people are free to take care of themselves first. This is an aspect of negotiating from strength. Often marriage promises create unequal footing where people become subservient or obligated. True commitment does not simply come from the rational mind or a marriage decision. It is discovered and not entirely chosen. By discovered I mean that commitment in its deepest form comes from the heart and is a feeling energy that is best expressed in the moment.

There is more passion and commitment in relationships that are open to freedom and spontaneity. Energy moves more freely when it is less defined. All those jokes about giving your horse a large pasture, or your dog a long leash, hold metaphysical truth. If you tell someone they have to do something, they resist. If you allow them to do something they love, their interest strengthens because of the freedom. The context of partnership opens up the relationship system and transcends the old archetype of marriage, while still holding the power of commitment.

Bringing the word obligation into this discussion can further expand these points. Obligation is an opposite of commitment. Commitment results in a strong presence and through that presence, it becomes a passionate, forward-moving energy. It is life's purpose being expressed with forward-moving energy into infinite possibilities. If we marry or commit from the rational mind, we lock our commitment into a system that is based on obligation. With the rigidity of obligation, the love is dampened.

Commitment is best felt in the present. If we feel it as a sweeping and all encompassing future decision, it can result in feelings of obligation. This is a key aspect of why it is actually healthy to realize that partnerships and marriages can be ended. This also affects how people treat one another. If it is understood that both parties have the freedom to leave the relationship, then they each have the power to negotiate from strength in order to create a nurturing relationship. If a husband or wife thinks of us as a possession, it can foster inequities where a dominant spouse may think they can control the relationship. This does not mean that security or promises are all bad; most people need to feel certain and secure. I am not suggesting that we be uncommitted or threaten our partners. It is important to differentiate between being an uncommitted free spirit who is trapped in avoidance and someone who limits the effects of the negative archetype of marriage by being committed in the present. We can be fully with our partners without possessing them.

Chapter 5
The Evolving Unconditional Partnership

The new archetype of marriage is the evolving, unconditional partnership. Describing this new archetype is like describing love; it's easier to describe what it isn't. The preceding thoughts about the old archetype are a decent beginning because embracing the new is better accomplished when you know the old issues through which you're working.

Unconditional partnership is about merging with another and at the same time having the freedom to be oneself. It is commitment and devotion that is coming from a choice, which is experienced in the moment. It is a union that feeds the soul: a present time experience of love and commitment. It is the power of feeling the love and commitment in the moment that carries it into the future. The moment is influenced by the past blessings that the relationship has given you, and it is influenced by its future promise. Commitment is a present time experience that what is here now is good enough to continue to want. Wanting it now is the key. One day at a time is not a cliché—it is a truth.

The new archetype of marriage is therefore ever evolving. It is not a commodity that will ensure future connection, safety, or security. It is a present-time love that gives without concern for receiving. It is unconditional love. Unconditional love is what you have to give after you have faced your essential aloneness in this world and comforted yourself. The new archetype is giving without concern for receiving in one moment and at the same time, it is caring enough about yourself to make sure you are receiving in another. It is not blindly giving yourself to another; it is caring for yourself in their presence. It is experiencing that the relationship serves you one day at a time.

The new archetype is not knowing. It is easier to be in the moment when you accept that there are many things that you do not know. Not knowing helps you embrace trust and let go of control. Not knowing keeps your heart opened. With increased trust, less control, and an opened heart, you become closer to the infinite, and your relationship has infinite possibilities.

Many couples benefit from opening to a spiritual perspective and ideas that include accepting a higher power in their lives. The way many religions encourage this just pulls people into negative archetypes. I think anything that helps people focus on needs and purposes that are beyond their own immediate physical agenda will help them transcend the negative archetypes and become more intimate. Service is the best example of this. By committing to and focusing on purposes, such as services that are greater than and beyond the immediate scope of a relationship, we can transcend the possessive tendencies of the negative archetypes. If making the world a better place is our purpose, we begin to treat our partner and ourselves as an individual whose needs are greater than just those that our relationship with them provides. In a partnership, we are committed to our lover as a friend, and we care about what they need and what is right for them beyond our own personal needs. If what they need takes them away from us, we can have increased acceptance of it because we love them and are committed to them. Commitment takes us beyond our own possession issues, and feeling our connection to a greater world helps this process.

Trusting life itself is a key to this. Notice how often the word trust is used in the area of marriage and monogamy. People say, "I can trust her." This use of the term comes from the possessive archetype. It's as if the subliminal message is "I can trust her to continue to be my possession." Real trust is between you and yourself, with life itself. Real trust is trusting that you are lovable and will always have meaningful relationships. The new archetype is trusting that whatever happens is for the best. If you are rejected, it could be a blessing. It could be the universe's way to carry you closer to a different and more ideal relationship.

When we try to make a certain relationship work, we are trying to possess the person. Trust involves knowing that you will have a successful relationship. You may have some uncertainty about with whom it might be, but you can feel trust in the uncertainty. Even in the middle of a great long-term relationship, trusting yourself and your own desirability are more important than trusting your partner. Trusting also means knowing that life itself is unbreakable, and things always work out.

This also applies to people who are single and looking for a relationship. Trust the universe to be your dating service. Also trust the purpose of being single; it can be a time where much depth can be developed. Being single is a great opportunity to feel good enough within yourself, as well as to feel that life itself is good enough by itself. You do not need a relationship to fix any personal problem. You are good enough the way you are, and life is good the way it is. It seems that learning this is a key to manifesting a successful relationship.

So the new archetype of marriage holds many relationship ideals. It is about loving yourself enough, and being strong enough within yourself, that you can actually commit to another and not just to what you can get from them. It takes this kind of strength to love unconditionally. In the new archetype, it is trust, love, and uncertainty that create security.

CHAPTER 6
MARRIAGE AS A LEGAL CONTRACT

It will help us release negative archetypes from our relationships and create the new archetype if we recognize that marriage is not a relationship. It is a legal contract. Marriage can be an aspect of almost any kind of relationship. We can have an arranged marriage that begins without love or familiarity. We can have a celibate marriage, a monogamous, or an open marriage, to name a few. Marriage is simply a legal contract that many people choose to add to an emotionally committed relationship. There is much to be gained in understanding this fact, and in separating a relationship from its legal status. First, it helps us respect same sex couples that are not yet able to legally marry in most states or countries. It also offers people who are entering into emotionally committed relationships and considering legal marriage a way to separate their legal and spiritual motives. Separating the motives can make it easier to focus on the spiritual ideals instead of unconsciously assuming that marriage gives them those ideals. Thirdly, understanding that marriage is a legal contract is also a good first step to help those already married separate from any undesirable marriage archetypes that have unconsciously entered into their relationship.

I am not against legal marriages. They offer some simple protections, and I would especially recommend them to those who plan to have children. In the event of a separation, a marriage contract is the most basic way to protect both children's and parent's rights. Without one, it could be difficult to receive child support, shared custody, or visitation. Other values can be explained by understanding that without the protection of legal marriage, our partner's family could control legal issues—including our partner's dying process.

Same-sex couples experience this in most states in our country today. Imagine your partner in the hospital on life support. Without a clear Living Will, it would be your partner's family that would dictate the doctors' decisions. If your partner died, your in-laws could change your locks and control your possessions. Without marriage, the same could happen to heterosexual couples. This does not mean that I recommend marriage contracts to appease these fears. The most basic point here is to view legal marriage as secondary to the relationship itself. There is value in postponing legal marriage until you metamorphose into the new archetype of marriage. This would mean not adding the legal contract of marriage to the relationship until the relationship has evolved into a solid partnership, where the sense of partnership would be primary and the legal aspects of marriage would feel secondary.

CHAPTER 7
MARRIAGE IS NOT A FIX:
DON'T GET MARRIED UNTIL YOU ALREADY ARE

Many people approach marriage as a fix or a means of obtaining something that the relationship currently lacks. Marriage is a legal contract that will not change or fix anything. Classic expressions of how people express the desire to use marriage to fix problems include the following: "He'll be monogamous after we get married," or "We can share financial resources after we get married," or "She'll drink less when we get married." Often the opposite seems to be the case; with the security of marriage, problems can get worse. Marriage itself will not resolve these issues, and I recommend that people get married only after their relationship has evolved to where they already feel married and do not expect the legal contract to make a difference.

There is a communication game couples can play to help look at this. It's called, "A difference marriage would make is...?" Bob and Mallie Mandel created this game in which partners take turns saying the question out loud over and over, and answering with the first thought that comes to mind. If no new answers come to mind, keep repeating the question. Initially, you might find that your answers indicate that marriage would make a difference. For example, you might answer, we would have more time together, I would help more with housework, or we would feel legitimate in the community. Or, even more extreme, you might feel that marriage would make you monogamous or more comfortable combining financial resources. The idea of the game is to see if you feel that marriage would make a difference. When your answers indicate that marriage won't make a difference ("We already are such and such"), and you still want to marry, it shows you that you accept and can commit to your relationship the way it is, and are not looking for marriage to be a fix.

A similar suggestion is not to get married until you fall out of love. Falling in love includes some euphoria and fantasy, where we are making our partner out to be even better than they actually are. We need them to be a good person and for the relationship to be successful, so we elevate them above reality. We do this to protect ourselves from vulnerable feelings, and so we can feel more secure in the world. Waiting to marry until we fall out of love means waiting until the fantasy euphoria has worn off and our feet are on the ground. This might also be felt as the reality phase of a relationship, not the fantasy phase. Proceeding with marriage at this point makes more sense because you're not set up for a let down after the fantasy wears off.

In spite of my suggestion that couples not marry as a fix, it is often people's experience that marriage does change things for the better. I feel this positive impact would more likely be experienced when the current state of the relationship is accepted first. By playing these games and wanting your relationship the way it is, you are in the moment and experiencing real success. If you get legally married at this point, you may feel some added innocence and legitimacy in your connection. It is as if no matter how progressive your thinking is, you are still influenced by deep old issues about living in sin, and marriage makes you feel more innocent and legitimate. Marriage for the right reasons can give you some positive archetypes to enjoy.

PART III

THE ANATOMY OF MONOGAMY: WHAT MAKES MONOGAMY DIFFICULT?

CHAPTER 8
NATURE VS. NURTURE:
A SERIES OF INTERCONNECTING VARIABLES

There is much said and written about whether monogamy is biologically natural or something that has evolved culturally because it is practical. It may be fruitful to ask ourselves if it is our biological or genetic nature to be monogamous, or is monogamy relatively new to our cultural needs and, therefore, new to our biological or genetic instincts. Has the history of survival on this planet led to different instincts for men and women? Are men biologically motivated on a deep level to fertilize as many women as possible? Are women motivated to be fertilized by a strong male specimen who can protect and provide for her children?

The term nature vs. nurture is the more casual lay term often used to distinguish between biological tendencies and those created by personal experience. If we take the position that men are genetically programmed to fertilize as many women as possible, we are saying that it is not a man's "nature" to be monogamous. If we take the position that a man is having an affair because his father did, or because society has conditioned him to do so to prove his masculinity, then we are saying that the key is "nurture"— that the way the man has been treated since birth has nurtured or taught him the behavior.

If you ask similar questions in an academic setting, the same issues are often discussed within the term essentialist vs. social construction. Essentialist or essentialism are terms used to express the same issues as nature. Is a man essentially non-monogamous? Or, has his genetic history brought him to a point where non-monogamy is part of his essence? Social construction argues in favor of the nurture side of the question. Have men been constructed by societal influences to be promiscuous? These terms are used to address a wide variety of social and gender issues. For example, have men been trained to be aggressive and play with trucks? Have women been trained to nurture children and play with dolls?

Human nature is influenced by both nature and nurture. We have tendencies that come from our nature or our genetic roots and tendencies that come from social conditioning. We evolve in both areas because they inform each other over time. In other words, our genetic roots are influenced by our ancestors' past social conditioning, and by the way we are nurtured or socially conditioned to be within this lifetime. The opposite is also likely the case. These genetic or historical roots shape our preferences and therefore our current trends as to how we socially condition people to behave. What is encouraging about this is that, as we make new choices, we are influencing both the psychological and biological gene pool.

Research has shown that girls really do prefer dolls and boys prefer trucks. Researchers have also demonstrated that these preferences are because of both nature and nurture. While I appreciate that research has been done to clearly articulate the influences of each side of the issue, I feel both arguments are compelling and that we are influenced by both nature and nurture. We have biological drives as well as more psychological drives that are based on our past experience or conditioning. This actually empowers us, because it encourages us to work with all issues as we try to create monogamous relationships.

I take the position that men have a "bull mentality," meaning that they are still influenced by a genetic history where they are driven to fertilize the "herd." It is as if part of man's contribution to the world is to survey the "herd" and make sure that everyone has been recently fertilized. Men also have psychological issues that might motivate them to have multiple relationships or affairs. These include things like proving their masculinity or repeating their father's patterns and having affairs because he did. A man could also have the opposite reaction to their father having affairs. It could motivate them to be monogamous and not want to repeat their father's adulterous mistakes or hurt their partner or children. The subconscious will either avoid or follow family tradition. We avoid our parents' mistakes to avoid the pains we felt, and we follow their mistakes in an unconscious attempt to understand them.

The most basic example of a woman's nature is that she might be primarily motivated by the need to nurture her children for the first four or more years. This is a nesting instinct that is very monogamous, but is also not necessarily sexual. This is perhaps the female issue that is the opposite of a man's bull mentality. The man is motivated to go fertilize others, and the woman is motivated to stay at home and nurture the children.

Other examples of women's nature might be to continue to have children to ensure the survival of the species or to have children with multiple fathers—particularly if they find a stronger, healthier man to father their children. Women may also have an essential drive to keep a man around to help protect and provide for the children. If a woman with school age children had an affair, we could view the affair as being influenced by the fact that the children are old enough to help protect themselves now, so it is safer for her to move on to another man.

Women, of course, also have conditioning that is both pro-monogamous and non-monogamous. We might agree that women have more pro-monogamous conditioning than men. At times, our current culture seems to shame women's promiscuity more than men's. A teenage girl with two lovers is often viewed as a slut; a boy with two might be seen as lucky or popular. Women also tend to carry more fear of unwanted pregnancies, which could add to monogamous tendencies. Women's non-monogamous conditioning would probably be similar to men's, including reactions to any family or social issue, such as not wanting to be trapped in a bad marriage or wanting to prove femininity or receive affection through sex.

Another set of arguments based on the nature perspective is that men's physical strength has historically taken them out of the home, while women's ability to breast feed has more often kept them home in the role of nurturer. For women, this speaks to some pro-monogamous points that are derived from the nature viewpoint, like the one previously mentioned in which women may be driven by the need to nurture young children. Men being needed to protect women and children results in some pro-monogamy tendencies, but it could also go against monogamy because they are often out of the house to do so.

Anthropologically, men were also needed to migrate. You could even argue that men's physical strength is still in need in today's culture or mindset and that this is reflected in their higher wages. At the time of this writing, research shows that "women are paid 77.1 cents for every dollar men get" (Institute for Women's Policy Research, September 2009, www.iwpr.org). If you are a heterosexual woman, this income discrepancy could be an aspect of your need for a man. But if men need women to nurture children, it is still possible to keep a healthy balance. It is good to recognize that we need each other, and that needing each other can create loyalty and result in monogamous tendencies.

Our sexual desires may have been impacted by the difference in physical strength between men and women. Man's greater physical strength results in men feeling more comfortable with sex and sexuality and in women feeling more cautious around men. Most people would agree that it is harder for a woman to rape a man than for a man to rape a woman. Men have been, and still are, a threat to women. This, combined with a man's bull mentality, could help us understand the stereotype in which women tend to resist men's sexuality.

Women are more used to fielding or defending themselves from a man's desire, whereas men are more apt to feel safe with sexual desire in general. Men can generally walk through the world without the sexual desires of others being a threat. Women are more likely to avoid their desires because admitting them could more easily lead to unwanted advances. In blunt terms, the history of rape, incest, molestation, and even unwanted pregnancy have resulted in women needing to defend themselves sexually. The history of rape could also suggest that women might be prone to marry for security rather than love. By getting married, a woman secures a protector who is more able to protect her from the unwanted advances of others. Men may marry for security and physical reasons, too, but I think an anthropological study of this would suggest that men feel more physically safe in the world, and their needs are in the area of desiring a woman's labor to care for himself and his children.

There is also a third question that combines the nature and nurture issues. There is evidence, which suggests that from a historical perspective, monogamy is relatively new. If monogamy has become more popular in recent history, has this created a social conditioning that has increased our genetic tendencies to be monogamous? It can be argued that humans have only sought intimacy in their marriages for about 100 years, and monogamy has only become important during this period. Even if you argue that monogamy has held some importance throughout civilization, from an anthropological perspective it takes a long time for history to impact genetics. Regardless, since civilization is relatively new, monogamy is also relatively new. In the end, we are influenced by everything and are motivated and driven by a wide range of biological and psychological issues, which intersect to make up our own individual anatomy of sexual desire and monogamy.

I sometimes feel very conflicted about my own non-monogamous sexual desires. There are times where I feel my bull mentality motivating me as I walk through a group of people, as if it's my duty to find and impregnate some neglected soul. Having this feeling, in contrast to an opposing psychological state of enjoying my commitment to my partner, can be quite confusing. I have found myself distracted by my inner bull's desire even when I was happily in a relationship, or was not seeking one. It has become fashionable to criticize men for being horny. To this I say, "Being a bull is a tough job, but somebody has to do it."

Women, how would you like to be distracted by an irrational need to fertilize others? We all need to empathize with ourselves for the possibility that we may be driven by a genetic nature that is not monogamous. If we seek to have successful monogamous relationships, knowing that the non-monogamous side of our sexual desire runs deep will help us work through the powerful feelings without losing sight of our preference.

It is also helpful to ask similar questions about low sex drive. We may have hormonal or other medical issues that can create low sex drive and seek any necessary support with the more biological side of sex. The medical profession has an increased understanding of the hormonal aspects of what I'm calling nature or genetic instincts. Note that I would not recommend that a driven male bull consider chemical castration to make it easier to walk through a shopping mall, but medical science does offer help for those whose lack of hormones is part of their low sex drive. Both men and women's hormones affect their sex drive. I've included in my bibliography books on women's health, including *Women's Bodies, Women's Wisdom*, by Christiane Northrup, and a definitive book on women's hormones and menopause, *Screaming to be Heard*, by Elizabeth Vliet. I don't want to exclude men from the hormonal equation. For example, I know there are times when men need to consider hormone therapy or other drugs.

Men are also not excluded from the nurture side of the low sex drive issue. It is not just women that avoid sex for emotional reasons. We tend to assume that if a man lacks sex drive or has erection problems, he needs a drug to fix it. Men also have emotional issues that affect their ability to feel safe getting aroused and benefit as much as women do from viewing their issues on both the biological and emotional levels.

My approach is to have empathy for our biological or hormonal tendencies, but to work with our own unique history and social construction, because aside from hormone therapies, our psychological state is really the only part of the equation over which we have much control. I have often felt as I worked through my issues with my father, mother, sister, and society that I was also changing my genetic structure, thus making monogamy easier for my children's children. It's hard to say how much our efforts will help future generations; it is possible that the genetic issue is so dominant that our efforts will only make small changes. Even if this is the case, our efforts are still important because they will benefit us as well as our immediate families. It is, however, good to view both sides of the nature vs. nurture issue as connected in this way. As we work through our psychological issues, they impact the biological and make it easier for us to continue on our monogamous path; it also becomes easier for our children, both psychologically and biologically, to do the same.

CHAPTER 9
CHRONICLE #1: MY PARENTS

It is my hope that as you have been reading, you have been thinking about your life and relationships and applying the ideas regarding nature vs. nurture to your self and your relationships. Next I would like to share with you part of my story as a means of further illustration and to give you ideas that may help you apply this information to yourself. Here is part of my story:

My sense is that my father was having affairs at the time of my conception. When I was two years old, my mother finally hired a private investigator and caught my father in the act. During the next two years, my parents went through a couple of near separations. Each time tensions eased when my father promised never to do "it" again. When my mother caught him again, she gave up and divorced him. The year was 1962, and we lived in suburban San Francisco.

As a schoolteacher and a chemical engineer, they were both well known in our neighborhood and local community. It was humiliating for my mother to go through a divorce in that suburbia, with adultery as a cause, and she went into a depression. As an empathic four-year-old boy, I sensed her pain and tried to comfort her. She has frequently told the story of the time when my father picked my sister and me up for a weekend visit and, sensing her pain and fear of losing my love, I went to hug her and whispered in her ear, "Don't worry, Mommy, I love *you*."

It was scary to be four and not know if my mother would be able to hold it together. Thus, my family system pushed me into the role of the surrogate spouse: I became a source of comfort and nourishment for my mother. I, of course, didn't put this all together until entering therapy as an adult. It was then that I also learned about the deep fear this instilled in me about my sexuality. It was as if my father's sexuality almost killed my mother, my sister, and me.

From that early age on, a large part of my focus became making sure my sexuality didn't hurt people—especially women. My life became organized around giving and nurturing and making sure I didn't cause others pain. A monogamous psychotherapist was born.

My secondary response to my parents' divorce was to become numb and learn how *not* to need. My sister responded a little more directly. She is three years older than I am and was seven when my parents divorced. She expressed fears of loss: If Dad could leave, maybe Mom would, too. I, on the other hand, dealt with my fear by taking care of others so they might be better equipped to take care of me. I also took little, disappearing and living down the street at a neighbor's house or at home in front of the television. I felt that if I didn't need anything then perhaps my mother and sister would be able to survive. My belief that it was best for me not to need certainly created major conflicts as I grew and became a sexual being.

My father and I had only one conversation about relationships with women, and it was hardly a "heart to heart." All he said was not to hurt women. This only added to the already existing negation of my sexuality. He said nothing about my desires being innocent or challenging. I think this is typical and valuable for men and women to note how this communication was also demeaning toward women: It assumes they are weak and cannot take care of themselves.

Also note that what the typical parent tells their daughter about boys does something similar. Our culture either subliminally or overtly tells young women that a boy's sexual advances may become a problem, and she needs to prepare herself to say no to him, but she is not shown or taught how to deal with her own desires. By encouraging our daughters to stay away from these "evil" advances of boys, we imply that they will have difficulty protecting themselves, that they are weak, and that they shouldn't have any problems with sexual desire because they have none. If we were to teach adolescent girls and boys that they have strong desires, and they will be happiest if they deal with their desires constructively, we foster much healthier sexual development.

I have since lived with these conflicts deep inside me: my sexual desires were wrong; it is best to give and not need; and certainly don't hurt women. As I grew, society further ingrained these precepts by pointing out that it would be bad to commit adultery. I was not imagining committing adultery at age fifteen, but growing up knowing that I had strong sexual desires and that there were so many rules about how sexuality could be expressed gave me a strong sense of pressure. I hoped I would be a good man and not hurt women. I lost much of my sexual innocence by worrying about this.

Both my parents dated and remarried. I can't say that my parents' dating processes had much effect on me or my sexuality except for the guy who kept wanting me to go to bed so he could get into my mother's pants. I finally did go to bed, but this time I whispered, "He is a bad man," as I hugged my mom goodnight. I suppose we all have some experiences that teach us that *men only want one thing.* This message poses a problem if you're a woman defending yourself from these supposedly evil advances. On the other hand, if you're a man the message you receive is that you are bad. This kind of shame about my sexuality and my pending testosterone-based sex drive should have led to a train wreck.

I was fortunate my stepmother, on the other hand, provided a positive influence. She guided me away from sexual guilt and was the only person who ever really talked to me about girls. When I was around thirteen years old, she wrote me a letter, and then we talked briefly. The main thing I learned from what she said was that I had desires that were normal. I don't know if I realized it at the time, but it was great to have an adult acknowledge that seeking a relationship with the opposite sex was stressful. She also gave me some simple tips about what girls liked. Overall, her communication was not about encouraging me to behave properly, as my father's guidance had been, but about validating that my needs were important. She wanted to help me fulfill my goal of having a successful relationship. This kind of support is rare even now, but was especially so for the times. She was one of the early personal growth seekers in San Francisco in the early '70s, and I credit her for injecting a vision that helped me to create successful relationships and find my career.

47

CHAPTER 10
LAWS OF ATTRACTION AND DESIRE

Next, I want to focus on the nature or social conditioning perspective by talking about the psychological and the metaphysical principles that govern what we attract and are attracted to in relationships. Understanding that our attractions and desires are driven by both our conscious and unconscious mind is an important first step to working through any relationship patterns, including the sexual patterns that affect our monogamy. The same principle applies to all relationships whether personal or business, significant or superficial. The universe is not as random as it sometimes seems. There are universal laws of attraction that can explain many abstract details of our life and relationships.

We attract events and people to our lives that fit our expectations. It is as if our beliefs, whether conscious or unconscious, act as metaphysical commands to the environment, and we end up having relationships with people who fit our beliefs. Our results in life reveal our subconscious expectations. It has often been said that, "Our results are our Guru"; they teach us what is unresolved in our thought patterns. In this way, negative results are the universe's way of forcing us to continue to resolve our past and its emotional impact.

For example, if someone has a pattern of attracting partners who are not monogamous, they might want to look at their abandonment or low self-esteem issues. There are many specifics that could fit here: They may have issues around feeling unwanted or that they didn't belong in the world, or more general issues of feeling that they are not good enough. For many people these issues relate back to their prenatal experience and can include feeling like a burden if there was financial stress, and gender identity issues if their parents wanted them to be a different sex. Ultimately, to resolve loss or self-esteem issues it is helpful to address any and all issues from our early life, including our own birth experience. Investigating and resolving the earliest doubts we had about being worthy of life and love is the key to letting go of the shame-based conditions that are receptive to loss and abandonment.

In addition to these specifics, our birth experience is often the deepest source of more generalized feelings of low self-esteem, rejection, and the belief that we are not good enough. Negative beliefs can be the result of something as simple as feeling rejected if we were separated from our mother at birth. In my case, I concluded that I must not be good enough when I was separated from my mother. This resulted in my expecting abandonment even though my parents planned to have me and they wanted a boy. All of these are details of a shame-based psyche and could be generalized further as low self-esteem issues. Low self-esteem can result in feeling that we don't deserve monogamy and can attract non-monogamous partners.

The same metaphysical principles govern an individual's tendency to be monogamous or not. An appropriate title for this aspect of this chapter might be the *Laws of Neurotic Desire*. What we choose in life is affected by our subconscious motivations. Sometimes the low self-esteem issues that can attract abandonment can also drive us to have relationships. Here the issue might be about proving we are wanted, that we are good enough or have value, are good enough as a man or woman, or that we are a contribution. Other terms I use to address this side of the equation are compensation or overcompensation. We tend to overcompensate to prove our worth by adopting perfectionist behavior. Having the drive or desire to prove ourselves can be a helpful motivation that pushes us out into the world to create success. However, if we are already in a monogamous relationship and still unconsciously seeking validation, we will tend to attract another partner with whom to prove ourselves. Perfectionism in the area of relationships can actually come out as a conquest pattern that moves individuals from one partner to the next.

There are three ways we attract or act out our patterns. The first is the *law of attraction*: We attract what we are expecting. This could mean attracting a partner who had affairs if our emotional state is receptive to that because of past abandonment issues or if we expected that people had affairs because our parents did. The second is the *law of interpretation*: We interpret or project what we expect whether it is true or not. This could mean interpreting our partner's occasional long hours at work as meaning that they must be having an affair. And the third law is *manifestation*: This points out how we can push others towards our expectations. The *law of manifestation* could mean driving a partner to have an affair, which we could conceivably do by any number of means, such as emotionally abusing them or by withdrawing from the sexual relationship. Granted, we can't make someone do anything, but we can behave in a way that is receptive to manifesting certain behaviors.

The laws of attraction, interpretation, and manifestation also tend to work together. Imagine Mary, who felt abandoned by her father when her parents divorced when she was a small child. She married and *attracted* a husband who had affairs and left her. After her divorce, she began to date, but her self-esteem and fear of abandonment were sensitive issues. If a man she was dating showed any indifference toward her or interest in other women, she would assume or *interpret* the man's behavior as him not being interested enough in her and that he could not be trusted. She developed a tendency to confront men for their lack of interest or their attraction toward other women. These conversations frequently led to upsets that would drive men that were interested in her away. If was as if she picked fights until she *manifested* her unconscious expectation. Her relationships revolved around the many ways she assumed that she would be rejected.

In the middle of this pattern, she couldn't objectively see if she had actually attracted someone who was disinterested or untrustworthy or whether she was interpreting or projecting the pattern. Unfortunately, when we are caught up in a pattern like this, we tend to behave in ways that manifest the pattern and our patterns become self-fulfilling prophecies.

An important aspect of understanding how we attract relationships is to understand that we don't need to change our partner or the tendencies of the female or male gender. All that is needed is to resolve our issues so that we become receptive to something new. Understanding the laws of attraction is empowering because they explain why we don't need to change people to get what we want; we just need to change our side of the pattern to attract someone else or to attract a different part of our partner.

Patterns are an equal mix of both people's issues interacting. They are always fifty-fifty. Metaphysically, patterns are 100 percent/100 percent. This means that on some level it's all us, because it is our half that is attracting and interacting with others. We are 100% responsible for our results: If our half wasn't there, we would have attracted a different result. We don't need to focus on the other person's half, just our own half that makes us receptive to theirs.

In the case of an existing partnership, if *we* change, the part of them that we are attracting will change. For example, if we are in relationship with someone who is a workaholic and we work through the abandonment issues that are receptive to it, their behavior will change or they will act out their issues in another area. Even if they don't resolve the issues that make them feel the need to work so hard, if we stop being receptive to the time apart, they will act out their issues differently. For example, they might take up therapy and work to have a better relationship with us.

Most people have a history of attracting a certain kind of person. For example, if you are a single man, and you have a history of attracting cold, unavailable women who leave you, you don't need to change women as a gender. You need to address the aspect of you that attracts cold women or abandonment. Most of us are only looking for one partner. Even if women on average were essentially more emotionally cold and unavailable than you, by resolving your own issues you would attract the warmth and lasting relationship you desire.

Notice that I reversed a common gender stereotype in this example. I did this to point out that gender stereotypes are not universal truths and that our own personal issues are always important to address. There are men who have believed women to be the more emotionally distant gender and have attracted negative experiences with women based on that belief. In fact, I was one of them. In the next chronicle, I describe the origins of my rejection and abandonment issues with women. These were my issues, and they say more about me than they do the female gender.

There are many ways to resolve patterns. One of the most basic is to distill them down to the unconscious beliefs that are driving the issue and change the beliefs. Changing the beliefs requires a multidimensional approach; beliefs are not simply held in our mind but also in our body, spirit, and emotions. Virtually every personal growth endeavor will include all aspects of being to a degree, but I recommend that our approach be as holistic as possible. I do not favor just sitting around making intellectual connections. The more time we can devote to the expression and movement of the feelings associated with our beliefs, the better.

That said, I frequently use affirmations in my work, and there are many mentioned throughout this book. An affirmation is a conscious thought that we choose to immerse into our subconscious mind in order to produce a desired result. When working with any psycho-spiritual issue, it helps to discover the operating beliefs and use affirmations to assist us in resolving the issue and change the behaviors associated with it. Keep in mind that I am also recommending more feeling based processes to accompany affirmations and the reversal of negative beliefs.

What is empowering about the laws of attraction is that no matter what we may have attracted in the past, we have the ability to resolve it, and can attract something new by focusing on ourselves and our 100% of the relationship. There are times when we need to face the reality that our partner has a problem from which we need to get away. For example, I wouldn't suggest you work on the issue of why you're in a physically abusive relationship; I would just get away from the danger and ask that question later. For the most part, we all need to get better at admitting our own issues and shifting the energies and beliefs we bring to relationships.

CHAPTER 11
CHRONICLE #2: ABANDONMENT AND LOSS

While many people's abandonment issues result in their avoidance of relationships, my own abandonment issues have driven me to compensate by seeking love and approval. Particularly as an adolescent and young adult, I was a seeker of love and went steady with eighteen girls from the ages eleven to seventeen. I don't have a memory of how many others turned me down, but I'm sure there were many. All but one of the girls I went steady with broke up with me, usually after two to four weeks. Each time I was devastated. As I grew and became more and more familiar with this pattern of seeking love and approval, followed by abandonment, I knew something was going on, and throughout my teenage years, I became more and more interested in spiritual and psychological explanations. I began to study the source of why I continued to create (or be in) relationships in which I was rejected or abandoned.

This process of exploration took a dramatic leap when my father died when I was nineteen. My parents' divorce and shared parenting was quite healthy for their time, and although I lived with my mother, I had always been in close contact with my father, especially as a teen. We were very close, and I would usually talk to him by phone every day and visit him at least once a week. Although he had shortcomings, he had also become a great father, teacher, and guide in my life. It was devastating to lose him as I grew into manhood; it brought up the pain of all the previous times in which I felt abandoned. I cried every day for a year, switched my college studies from philosophy and business to philosophy and psychology, and I began counseling and taking workshops to help me resolve the various losses in my life.

I spent three months that next summer as a work scholar at Esalen Institute in Big Sur, California. Esalen is one of the original personal growth retreat centers and remains a Mecca for personal growth education. I was searching for the alternative therapies that would be right for both my budding career and my personal growth. I received tremendous value from everything at Esalen, and it was there that I had a rebirthing/breathwork session for the first time. Breathwork was the process I was looking for—it provided great release and spiritual connection, something I needed after the year of grief and anger I had experienced.

I explain breathwork in more detail later, but I'll introduce it briefly here. Originally called rebirthing, breathwork involves breathing in a full, free manner (as guided by a trained facilitator); the result is an increase in the level of physical and spiritual energy in the body, thus cleansing the many tensions held there. The result of the physical cleansing is that the mental and emotional origins of tension come back into consciousness and can then be healed. By learning to breathe consciously and fully, we discover and release the core issues held in our mind and emotions. When Leonard Orr developed rebirthing in the early '70s, both he and his first clients relived their births, discovering the tremendous impact birth had had on them. Rebirthing has since undergone many changes to become a more holistic process, addressing our entire childhood and life experience. Many rebirthers have changed the name from rebirthing to breathwork, but understanding the birth experience remains one of the valuable results.

Please note: Rebirthing/Breathwork is always about breathing fully and freely and never involves pushing a client through a tunnel of blankets and pillows or otherwise re-enacting the birth process. The term rebirthing was incorrectly used by therapists to describe a completely different process that involved trying to re-create the birth process/experience, which resulted in the death of Candace Newmaker, an eleven-year-old girl, in 2000. Outside of these isolated therapists, and this isolated tragedy, rebirthing is always breathwork that occurs freely in open air.

During the next few years of intensive therapy and training as a rebirther and counselor, I discovered a whole host of issues that combined to make up my abandonment issues and quest for love and approval, especially from women. The first big ah-ha came during a rebirthing session when I spontaneously relived an aspect of my birth in which I remembered the sadness and loneliness of being separated from my mother. As I felt the pain of this separation, which I interpreted as abandonment, it was as if my whole life made sense. I said to myself, "That's why women leave me—I expect them to." Our past creates subconscious beliefs and expectations, which continue to regenerate similar people or events in our lives. Gaining awareness of this belief that "women leave me" helped me begin to release the energy and issues associated with it. At that point, my rejection issues with women began to shift.

The next big layer was peeled back when I realized that my sister didn't want me. I pieced together a variety of memories that were representative of that realization, such as the time when after a day at the beach she had asked my mother if "we could leave him here." This gave me additional clarification about my abandonment issues with women.

Yet another step came when I added my experience of my parents' separation, and how I felt abandoned by my father when my parents divorced. These three events combined to explain my track record with rejection and explained the loss I sought to resolve by seeking love. Someone with the same story could have easily retreated into withdrawal and protected him or herself by avoiding relationships or commitment.

As I worked through these issues, my relationships with women shifted, and my results changed to a more even mix, where sometimes relationships changed or ended because of my choices and sometimes because of the choices made by my partner. I felt free. I began to have my own identity and opinions about whether or not a relationship suited me, as opposed to purely being motivated to create a connection anywhere I might get some of my needs met.

CHAPTER 12
OPPOSITES ATTRACT:
UNDERSTANDING PRIMARY AND DISOWNED SELVES

The previous model expresses how we re-create past traumas and unconscious beliefs. Another lens I use helps us understand how opposites attract. Here I study how our position or energy attracts its opposite in others.

Many relationship models address how opposites attract in various ways and to various degrees. I do not discuss opposites to focus on gender stereotypes. I prefer to see our tendencies as individual issues that go beyond gender. Each individual is unique and will attract or be attracted to their unique opposites. Whatever our position or personality we will likely feel that a variety of energies are different or opposite it. For example, if we are strong and are invested in being strong we will be drawn to (or repulsed by) not just weakness but also the qualities of vulnerability, spontaneity, and emotion as well. The opposite of financial security can be poverty, vulnerability, or spontaneity. Spontaneity could be felt as an opposite of the well-controlled personality that is focused on financial security. Opposites of sexually open or interested can be celibate, authoritative, controlling, or organized. The opposite of old is not just young; it can be youthful, immature, spontaneous, or free. The opposite of unemotional is not only emotional but also childlike, passionate, artistic, and sexual. The opposite of emotional is not just suppressed; it can be strong, rational, or parental.

The deepest explanation I have found as to how opposites attract is in the work of Hal and Sidra Stone and the Voice Dialogue process they created. Voice dialogue is based on a "psychology of selves" approach to personal development. It assumes we can obtain greater clarity and freedom of choice when we begin to understand that our psyche is composed of various selves or sub-personalities, each with different roles and purposes in our lives. These selves can also be thought of as energies or personality characteristics.

As we become more aware of how selves are operating in our lives, it is helpful to distinguish them as either "primary selves" or "disowned selves." The term "primary self" refers to our primary ways of being. We have an inner value system or inner rules that govern our preferred way of being, and these rules are followed and implemented by selves that express their values. One way primary selves are formed is by inheriting, or rebelling from, the value systems to which we are exposed, most often from our family experience. Some common examples of selves we might have: a "pleaser" self to follow the rule "be nice"; a "pusher" self to honor a work ethic; and a "controller/protector" to protect us from being hurt. If selves are formed in rebellion to the primary culture of our family, they could also be expressing values such as "be irresponsible," "play first," or "rest often," but this is less common.

The term "disowned self" refers to personality traits or energies that an individual either does not cultivate or tries to eliminate from their life and personality in order to maintain a primary self's way of being. For example, if your family ethic was "work hard" and you conform to this by having a strong pusher, you will naturally disown or avoid the opposite energies of playing, resting, or laziness. This is a good description of the use of the term "shadow." The opposite of our primary self is our shadow, and we work to avoid it.

Viewing relationships via our primary and disowned selves offers a powerful way of describing the energies or personality characteristics we are likely to be attracted to or repulsed by in others. When we say that opposites attract, it means that if we are carrying a particular energy we will likely be in a relationship with someone who is carrying the opposite energy. When we have negative reactions to people, our reaction can be explained by how the person or event differs from our primary self. For example if you have a primary self of being a good and nurturing friend who is a good listener, people who are self absorbed and talkative may upset you more than they would upset someone else. People whose primary selves differ from ours can be felt as our shadow, and we may be reactive to them.

Even our reactions to news events can be explained by which disowned self the news triggers in us. While negative events are upsetting to nearly everyone, we all have different hot buttons. For example, some of us are more offended by stories about neglectful or abusive parents, others by stories of governmental abuses of power, and others by stories of unemployed people or welfare fraud. The prior model about the laws of attraction explains this by identifying how we react to things because they remind us of past hurts. The abusive parent or authority, or the unemployed, may be a re-creation or projection of an old family or childhood wound. From the view of how opposites interact, our reactions are not just based on wounds; they are based on the cultural bias of our primary self. Our primary self tends to judge people who are different.

The difference between a positive and negative reaction can be explained by noting that when we feel threatened by a difference, we react negatively, and when we feel freed by one, we react positively. If a difference offends our identity and investment in our inner culture, we will resist it. If our inner culture likes the difference because it makes us feel more whole, balanced, or stable we will be attracted to it. Another specific aspect of this theory is that we are likely to be attracted to energies we lack or have disowned from our lives. We will tend to be attracted to potential partners who have an energy from which we feel disconnected. The system of our inner world craves stability and draws people to us whose strengths differ from our own. Understanding opposites as differences may be helpful. We are attracted to differences that help us feel expanded, balanced, and whole.

All aspects of life and personalities are valid. There is not just one correct way to live. While we may have our own preferred ways of being, it is as if the universe sends us additional ideas so we can learn from them and become more whole. It is healthier for us if we can develop all aspects of ourselves; meeting people who are different from us gives us the opportunity to develop the other parts. Initially these differences are a source of increased balance, and we will tend to like the feeling. Later, when more stress enters a relationship, we will tend to flip our position from liking the differences to judging them. Originally, our primary self likes its opposite, and later it tends to judge it for being different. Embracing differences and learning from them will help in all phases of a relationship.

This also describes one big problem in the world of relationships and world peace. We tend to stay too identified with our primary self's culture and tend to be scared and judgmental of those who are different. Many chronically single people end relationships at the point where the differences are a source of conflict instead of continuing to embrace and learn from the other's perspective. The first settlers of the United States were very different from the Native Americans who already inhabited the land. If the Indians had not been gracious enough to teach the pilgrims how to live on the land, the pilgrims would have died. In the beginning, the differences were welcomed, but as time went on the pilgrims became less comfortable with them. World politics may be similar; if we listened to and learned from each other, we would become more diverse, thus becoming more secure and stable. We would be more able to sustain and evolve in various conditions.

The same is true in personal relationships. I see the universe's most personal goal for us as learning to become whole and comfortable with all of the energies within it. This applies to our relationships with others and to our relationship with ourselves. The infinite wants us to be comfortable with all of us, and it sends us different kinds of people so we can learn that all of us are okay. It is miraculous when we take a problem we are having with another and let go of our own righteousness and embrace their way. Not only does the conflict subside but we also become more of who we really are; we become more infinite ourselves. The universe can teach us that we are more than our favorite selves; we are everything.

CHAPTER 13
CHRONICLE #3: BEING ATTRACTED TO MY DISOWNED SELVES

I was twenty-three years old when I met my ex-wife Paula. I was on a very responsible career track. Although by many standards I was "going on forty" with maturity and career success, I was also fueled by the insecurity of a twenty-three-year-old. I had always had a very responsible primary self—an energy I needed to create a safe and secure world.

When I was first attracted to Paula, I was seeking a secure and responsible marriage and was attracted to her equally grounded and responsible nature. As we built our life together, we regularly increased our stability and security, as well as our responsibilities. The primary self of our marriage was that of being responsible. We each had different areas in which we carried the responsibility for the success of the family, but we each pushed and worked quite hard. While the success that goes with this was a major goal for each of us, as time went on, we both began to pay the price of the disowned self of our relationship. The disowned self of our relationship contained the qualities opposite to that of responsibility: rest, play, "being-ness" and yes, sexuality.

Whether it is conscious or not, most people have the desire for increased success and security as one of their primary goals for marriage. As they focus on being responsible, they ironically push away qualities and activities such as sexuality and playfulness, qualities that also add to the aliveness and stability of the marriage. It is all too common to hear a person who is working hard to make their marriage a "success" sarcastically joke, "Who has the time or energy for sex?" The pressure Paula and I shared to be responsible, and our emerging desire for rest and play, took various forms and resulted in a variety of conflicts.

Although it was quite subconscious, my desire to have a more free and relaxed experience fueled my tendency to fantasize about and desire other women. Theoretically, given my situation, and using the theories of voice dialogue, I would have been drawn to free spirits, or women who more noticeably embraced their sexuality. For me, this was partly the case, but my tendency to desire authoritative women remained, as well as increasingly being attracted to women whom I imagined to be nurturing and sexual. Again, this is because in the push for our marriage to be a source of security and strength, the more nurturing, free, or sexual energies had become disowned.

During my sixteen-year marriage, I would occasionally meet someone to whom I felt extremely attracted. In most of these cases, I didn't have enough contact with the person for the attraction to develop very deeply. Even if I approached them to discover what the attraction represented or what I needed in my life, I always kept things distant enough to "ensure" that I wouldn't have an affair. Looking back, there are two women that posed a significant challenge to my sense of stability in my marriage. In both of these cases, the process of confronting and embracing the "disowned" energy that I was lacking and desiring in my life was instrumental in dealing with these challenges.

The first experience was with Sharon. I met Sharon in 1989, when I traveled to another city to attend a seminar for my own personal growth. I had traveled frequently without Paula over the years, but usually I was in the role of the teacher—a role that gave me an additional buffer from my attractions. Early in this intensive weekend workshop, which had around fifty people in attendance, I noticed Sharon, a very attractive woman. Using one of my older tools, I tended to avoid her.

Despite my desire to avoid Sharon, as the workshop progressed, we had increased contact and did some pretty powerful exercises together. I was having feelings of deep love and attraction to the disowned self, which Sharon represented to me: gentleness, peace, nurturing, and sexuality. Though infatuated, I remained committed to keeping my distance from her. The next day there was a point where it was appropriate to mention this, which I did, and this helped me to release my phobia and resume normal relations. Nevertheless, my attraction remained.

The main thing I learned from my attraction to Sharon was that I wasn't getting the sexual connection I needed in my marriage. I did some work on this by trying to create and embrace those qualities within myself and within Paula, but with a three-year-old and another child on the way, it didn't feel appropriate to push my sexual needs onto Paula at the time. I continued to disown my sexual desire and focus on the responsible side of our life together.

Throughout the following years, I continued to have and embrace my attractions along similar lines. Paula and I continued to grow apart sexually, and I did little to confront it. In 1994, I went back to school in hopes of going to graduate school and increasing my professional authority within academia. (Although I was already an internationally known counselor and teacher in the field of relationships, my authority was based on the personal growth seminar traditions. In these traditions, acknowledgment from your peers and from your students was held above that of academia or state licensing.)

My being in school only accelerated the friction between Paula and me, as we felt the burden of an even more stressful schedule. That year I met Patricia, the second woman who exposed my disowned needs. She was the facilitator of some classes I attended. She was older, and in my projection of my disowned self, I was attracted to her gentleness, kindness, and nurturing personality. I realized I must deeply need these qualities, and I developed a "crush" on her.

I had ongoing contact with Patricia. I took four classes from her over the period of a year, and we had coffee together several times. This was the first time I had extended contact with someone with whom I was deeply attracted. I was able to resolve my crush on her by the end of that year. By admitting it fully to myself and remaining in contact with her, I began to see her for who she really was. She became someone I liked but not someone with the all-encompassing nurturing qualities I had envisioned. I also accepted that I needed to solve my nourishment issues on my own.

My relationships with Sharon and Patricia helped me to admit and work through what was lacking in my life in a general way. Looking specifically at the disowned selves involved also helped me to work through the issues deeply and connect with the details of my nourishment and marriage issues. Clearly, it was not just more sex and nurturing that I craved in my life. Sharon and Patricia helped me realize that I needed to create more tenderness, freedom, and mothering in my life, both from within and in my relationships.

Opposites Attract: Understanding Primary and Disowned Selves Continued

We all need to be aware of the "selves" or the qualities to which we are attracted in people. This could be quite general. For example, if we are attracted to almost everyone, we might conclude that we just crave connection or sex, and this would help us confront what is lacking in our life in a general way. Or, if our attractions are more specific, we may be able to become aware that the people to whom we are attracted share a similar energy. This enables us to see that the subject of our attraction represents a specific energy that is missing from our lives, and we can then take steps to create that energy within our relationships or within ourselves.

For example, if we are in a partnership and are attracted to people we feel to be free spirits, we can take steps to make our relationship less bound by responsibility and more based on rest, play, spontaneity, or sexuality. If we are attracted to physical people, we can incorporate more physical activity into our lives or relationships. If we are attracted to intellectual or responsible people, we can work to develop intellectual or responsible aspects.

Single people can work with the same principles and become more conscious of what drives their attractions. They may decide which attractions they want to pursue in their life. For example, if someone ends a relationship with a person who was too much of a free spirit, they will likely crave stability when they date again. If they then unconsciously enter a relationship with someone who is too conservative or suppressed, they will likely regret that later. People tend to "flop" from one problem to another. If they instead create a balance by working on these issues within themselves, they will be better able to create a relationship that meets more of their needs.

Another powerful example can be found among people who are recovering from abusive or chaotic childhoods. It is quite common to apply the previous model of attraction and say that abuse survivors re-create abuse in their lives because they are familiar with it. I find that it is equally common for people to be attracted to the opposite of their past, and that individuals with chaotic or abusive childhoods will often be attracted to, and form relationships with, stable, grounded people. This can lead to problems later in the relationship when the value of the stability wears off and it is instead felt to be suppression, avoidance, or non-communication. Once stability becomes the primary system, people are more likely to yearn for someone who is more spontaneous, emotional, or sexual.

I certainly recommend stability over chaos or abuse, but seeing this issue can help people whose fear of abuse has resulted in an unnecessary attachment to stability. Letting go of the attachment to stability can help them open to spontaneity, freedom, and liveliness in their relationships.

It is important to work with our disowned selves inside

ourselves and avoid the temptation to expect our partner to fulfill all of our needs for a particular energy. If we develop the energy within ourselves, we gain peace and inner stability whether or not we actually receive the quality within our relationship. We will also be more likely to receive this energy from our partner. Our partner will feel more able to tap their own disowned energies because they will not feel as pushed by us. Also, if we connect with an energy on an inner level and don't force it on our partner, we become a leader and our partner will be more able to follow. By holding an energy within, we can attract, foster, and induct it from our partner. If we push our partner to be the leader, they are more likely to feel criticized by us and resist.

This is theoretically true even with sexuality. If our relationship lacks the sex we desire, and we are attracted to people we perceive to be more free and sexual, the first step is for us to get in touch with our own sexuality. If we resolve our own less sexual aspects and get more authentically in touch with our sexual nature, we will become more balanced. Getting in touch with our sexual nature and innocence is inner work—it will be an inner focus, which is felt on the inside and not necessarily easily measured by external appearances. Any arena that helps us address and discuss our awareness of ourselves as sexual beings should help us get in touch with our sexuality. This is a basic purpose of this book; the act of reading it will help us focus on our selves as sexual beings.

Discussing sexual issues with friends or counselors would enhance the process further by taking sexual taboos out of the shadows of our lives, helping us to embrace our sexuality as innocent. Being able to enjoy ourselves as sexual beings will result in us being less likely to crave attention from people other than our partner. When we are in touch with our sexual innocence, our partner will be more likely to desire us. By becoming more deeply in touch with our sexual side, we will meet many of our sexual needs on an inner level, and the tendency to be attracted to highly sexual people will subside.

Getting in touch with our sexual side can occur with or without sex. By embracing our sexual nature as a self or a group of needs (or selves), we can have greater connection with our sexual side. We will also become more aware of other needs—such as nurturing, comfort, self-esteem, and desirability—that are connected to our sexuality and become better able to meet those needs within ourselves. By deepening our relationship with ourselves in this way, our partner will be more likely to confront their sexual issues and become more comfortable with their own love and sexual desire. This is the case partly because if one person has disowned their sexuality in a relationship, the other has probably accommodated them by becoming sexually avoidant. By becoming more sexual and intimate within ourselves, we are taking responsibility for bringing increased sexual energy into the relationship.

This also means that highly sexual people will need to contact their non-sexual side. By embracing the part of themselves that is scared of sex, too shy, or doesn't want that much intimacy, they will stop pushing so hard for sex because they will be in touch with both sides of the issue. Being in touch with both sides of the issue creates true freedom and openings for both partners. It makes us less one-dimensional, and there is more space for change and movement. Shyness and non-sexuality are universal energies that we all have. They are as important as our sexual nature. To be sexual in a deep way, we actually need awareness of our non-sexual side. If both parties in a relationship are expressing these softer aspects of themselves, as well as their more raw sexuality, the relationship will have greater equal flow, back and forth, between sexual and non-sexual intimacy.

It may feel like a risk to embrace our own sexual nature. Moving toward our own sexual desire will be risking rejection because our partner may not join us. Being willing to risk rejection is central to having relationships and increasing the intimacy within them. If we don't embody our own desires and goals, there is almost no chance that our partner will. Someone has to take the first step. Taking these steps may expose that our partner is unable or unwilling to join us, but we need to take them for ourselves and for our own healing.

This suggestion is quite different from pushing our sexuality onto our partner. This is an important distinction because often the less sexual person in a relationship already feels overwhelmed by the other's sexual advances. The less sexual person reading this could hear me suggesting that their partner express even more sexual desire, which could result in them feeling even more defensive around sex. What I am saying instead is that the person in the more sexual role work further on the inner level to embrace his or her own sexual innocence. This results in fewer sexual overtures and greater sexual presence. By sexual presence, I mean having sexual energy without necessarily expressing it.

If our sexuality is strong and contained within ourselves, it expresses confidence that will make us more desirable. When we always pursue, we exude a needy expectation that is less attractive. When we hold our own sexual presence within, we release the expectation that the other should fulfill our need, and we become more desirable. Having this kind of sexual presence leads to greater intimacy because sometimes the overtures merely serve to keep things polarized into the roles of sexual aggressor and sexual resistor.

Another important aspect of this process is that by working internally to embrace a disowned self, our partner will become freer to move out of his or her side of the issue. For example, if we have a partner who is highly responsible and isn't playful or sexual enough for us, if we were to work harder and become more responsible, it would help our partner to let go of that role. Sometimes our partner is carrying a specific energy because they feel that someone has to, and if we help them carry it, they will lighten up. *Attention one-income partnerships: these principles apply to all kinds of responsibilities.* It's hard to feel playful, restful, or sexual when we are being responsible fifteen hours a day, even if those responsibilities are all domestic. Many couples find that it's easier to work outside the home than it is to run the household.

Using a non-sexual example of how couples tend to be opposites may help to create a deeper understanding of these dynamics. Couples are also frequently polar opposites in the area of money. This was the case with my ex-wife and me; we had a common set of opposing selves in our financial life. I was a spender and she was a saver. Initially, as our relationship developed, these opposites were forces of attraction just as with any aspect or self. She was attracted to the freedom and spontaneity of my spending and generosity; and I was attracted to the stability and security of her saving.

These differences were not a source of major stress early in our relationship because we each enjoyed the increased freedom and stability that the other's position gave us. Her interest in saving and investing discretionary income gave me a sense of increased abundance and self-worth. Conversely, my interest in having valuable experiences like vacations or desirable possessions helped her to increase her sense of pleasure, feeling of importance, and belonging in the world. As time went on, we still had problems in spite of our working to embrace each other's point of view. As our stresses entered the picture, we became more critical of our differences.

As stated before, early in a relationship, someone who is opposite our primary self can be freeing, but later in the relationship, we are more apt to criticize anything that differs from our primary self. Each person needs to embrace the value of each other's primary self. If the saver learns to spend early in the relationship, and the spender learns to save early in the relationship, a partnership will be more successful in all areas.

An important point in voice dialogue or a psychology of selves approach is that what initially is attractive to us because it is different or opposite, later becomes something that we resent because it is cramping our style and is felt to be oppressive. To dispel this feeling of oppression and resentment requires that the polarization be shifted by at least one of the partners leaving his or her position and embracing the other's position. In the case of the saver and the spender, the saver needs to relax, let go of responsibility, and spend more. The spender needs to become more responsible and spend less. When you to embrace your partner's way of being, you will grow, and they will feel seen and heard and will extend greater love to you as a result.

So, if your partner likes touch, touch them. If your partner likes restaurants, take them out and pay for it from your pocket. If your partner is worried about money, spend less. If your partner wants more sex, find and choose the part of you that enjoys it. If your partner is tired, help them with their chores. These examples are obvious, but the theories above should give deeper insight into the principles that govern this. Although doing this creates increased harmony and intimacy, the actual purpose is not to earn your partner's love. The deeper purpose is for you to grow and incorporate the disowned self that you attracted in your partner. It is for your growth that you let go of resisting your partner's ways of being.

CHAPTER 14
THE PRINCIPLE OF DESIRE

We have already explored how our desires have unconscious components that need to be more consciously resolved; however, desire is a very important and valuable thing. It is part of our life urge and is a sign of strength and vitality. Desire itself does not lead us away from monogamous relationships. It is a positive thing that makes monogamy easier, because when we have desire we are more likely to stay on course in a relationship and continue to manifest the intimacy we want. It takes strength and courage to have desire because when we express what we want, we are risking rejection. If we all played it safe and didn't express desire, relationships wouldn't form in the first place. If all partners played it safe and no one made the first move, then we would all be celibate or would never have been born in the first place.

It takes strength to have desire. We're risking failure when we admit that we want something. To continue wanting requires the strength to love ourselves if we fail or are rejected. Rejection is too painful to tolerate if we can't love ourselves or "self soothe" to repair our self-esteem if we lose the love we sought. Having the strength to face loss

I am complete — I don't need or want anything from you — I love you for your completeness & love sharing our vulnerabilities

or repair from loss are essential if we are to have and express desire. This is a deep aspect of why self-esteem is important for successful relationships, and self-soothing is an important aspect of self-esteem.

While I have always addressed this in my work, I first heard the phrase self-soothing from Dr. David Schnarch. Dr. Schnarch is a marriage counselor who shares a good and progressive relationship model in his books *Passionate Marriage, Constructing the Sexual Crucible* and *Resurrecting Sex* (see Suggested Readings). I feel his term self-soothing speaks to many universal therapy goals, including increasing self-esteem, comforting our inner-child, as well as connecting with our own power and autonomy. Self-soothing implies that we are powerful adults, capable of wanting, capable of repairing, and capable of figuring out how to do that. Self-soothing involves any aspect of self-care, such as taking a bath or a walk, exercising or eating well, or rewarding ourselves with rest or pleasure. More importantly, self-soothing is about the process of nurturing and loving ourselves at an inner level. It is about the psychology of developing strong, nurturing inner parent voices that help to balance the negative talk of the inner critic. Breathwork and Voice Dialogue are my two favorite tools for this.

Breathwork is a breathing process that creates a physical and emotional release that leaves people feeling free of negative self-talk and connected to their divinity. It is cellular self-soothing. Voice Dialogue works with the inner-child and inner parent selves at a deep level and helps people increase the presence of inner parent selves to soothe their inner-child. I'll discuss these tools in more detail in part V.

It also requires a lot of strength and desire to remain in a long-term relationship. The longer we are with someone, the more we rely on their presence, and the more difficult it would be to adjust to life without them. The more interdependent we become with a partner, the more we need them. If we do not possess the strength to want, we will protect ourselves emotionally by numbing out or by leaving the relationship. Abandonment is not only physical; it can also be emotional or spiritual. The fear of loss is part of why many couples emotionally abandon each other and live together in a dead relationship. Low self-esteem and the inability to self-soothe are deep reasons that many couples live in a state of withdrawal from each other, and it also explains a key reason that people leave relationships. It is as simple as we leave them before they can leave us. This also affects intimacy and sexual intimacy. It takes courage to sexually desire partners, both initially and long term. It could be our fear of loss that keeps us from having intimate sex with the one we live with.

As a couple matures in age, the issue of death enters the picture. Having a long-term relationship requires that we face the likelihood that one of us will die before the other. The fear of having our partner die is usually suppressed, especially when we are young, but it actually explains one reason people (of any age) end relationships. To enter long relationships, we need to have the strength to deal with all loss, including death. Facing the prospect of our partner going away is part of staying in love. Many marriages deal with this by just becoming emotionally distant so that if loss occurred, it would not be as painful. Since it takes strength to be alone, it also takes strength to continue loving and being intimate with our partner.

CHAPTER 15
HIGH AND LOW DESIRE PATTERNS

Another key issue is that if one person in the relationship is more comfortable expressing desire or has more in the first place, a couple can become polarized into roles in which one carries the desire and the other carries the resistance or ambivalence. This is an aspect of how opposites are attracted to each other and how we tend to attract someone who is the opposite of our primary self. The same principle can play havoc with the desire patterns in a relationship.

First, attracting opposites could result in people with two different desire patterns being attracted to each other. In purely sexual terms, a person with high sexual desire will be drawn to a person that they would unconsciously perceive to have the stability of being more reserved or having less sexual desire. The person with less sexual desire would conversely be attracted to the enthusiasm of the person with higher sexual desire. Later in the relationship, when the newness is over, these two are destined to have sexual conflict.

Their conflict will be exacerbated even further because a basic principle of desire is that the person with higher desire will force the other into resistance by pushing their desire upon them, and the person with lower desire will leave the high desire person stuck in desire by not being able to express it. If one partner is holding more desire, the other will have difficulty in finding their own desire, because they will be spending their time reacting to the other. They will end up criticizing the other for always being too sexual or not sexual enough.

Take Steve and Jennifer, a couple who were originally attracted to each other in part because they each possessed some similar opposites to those I mentioned in prior chapters. Steve had played hard in life and was now ready to settle down and be more responsible. Steve had a good job, worked hard, and had a strong sex drive. Jennifer was also ready to settle down, and stability had always been important to her, in part because her childhood was a little chaotic. Jennifer had always been more of a cautious and reserved person. She enjoyed sex, too, but was less overtly driven by it. Jennifer possessed a refined nature that Steve needed and was very attracted to. Jennifer was also very attracted to Steve's more expressive and playful nature, which she needed in her life. These opposites were a simple but strong source of attraction, and they fell in love and got married. As life together progressed and stresses mounted, the newness and fantasies wore off. These simple differences predisposed Steve and Jennifer to become polarized into a "high" and "low" desire pattern.

As Jennifer reverted to her more cautious primary self, she became less infatuated with Steve's more expressive and sexual nature. As Steve reverted to his primary self of being playful and sexual, he became more judgmental of Jennifer's more cautious and less sexual side. As this polarization grew, each felt criticized and defensive about their sexuality. Steve felt rejected and judged for wanting sex, and Jennifer felt pressured and judged for not wanting sex more often. Steve wanting sex so often made Jennifer want it less. She was so busy reacting to his advances that she became further polarized into her low desire. She could not feel her desire for Steve because it was as if she was always being chased. The more Steve felt rejected, the harder he pursued. It was as if Steve was always leaning forward to try to get sex, and Jennifer was always leaning back, reacting to feeling controlled or suffocated by his advances. Steve criticized Jennifer for never initiating sex, and Jennifer criticized Steve for never giving her room to initiate it.

To break this pattern, Steve had to let go and stop pursuing sex. He had to learn to self-soothe. Jennifer had to find her sexual nature and pursue Steve. It was hard for Steve to let go and touch Jennifer less because he felt such strong desire for her. It was hard for Jennifer to find her interest when she was so caught up in rebelling from Steve's advances.

In counseling sessions with me, they were able to talk about this and come up with some plans to correct this polarization. Steve agreed not to initiate sex for an indefinite period. I told him it might take months and that Jennifer may never want to have sex with him, but he was going to have to deal with it and self-soothe. Jennifer agreed to initiate sex when she wanted to. They both agreed to increase non-sexual intimacy and touching. They also agreed that if they did become sexual that either of them could stop at any point. This is critical: you won't feel free to start if you don't feel free to stop. Most people in

Jennifer's position resist kissing because they fear it will lead to foreplay, and they resist foreplay because they fear it will lead to intercourse. It is important not to worry about the high desire person being left hanging. Steve would rather have some loving touch with Jennifer than none, and he was okay with stopping. Steve also agreed to let her take and keep the lead on how far things went.

Notice what a healing role reversal this is even beyond the sexual arena. Steve was going to try to let go of controlling things by initiating, and Jennifer was going to claim her power and let go of being in the submissive or reactive position. This could teach Steve to receive and not have to be the guy who did so much. Jennifer could learn that she was worthy of being a leader.

At first these suggestions did not work. Steve said, "She's still withdrawn and doesn't want to be close or be held." Jennifer said, "He's still hovering over me asking me if I would like my shoulders rubbed." They were both trying to do it right, but Steve was not energetically letting go and Jennifer was not energetically "coming out." I pointed this out, and we did more work on the feelings underneath the issues. Both of them felt unworthy of love, which Steve expressed by chasing and Jennifer expressed by shutting down. Steve found self-soothing difficult and was more comfortable in the chasing/predator/hunter role. Jennifer had unresolved fear and anger from all the unwanted advances she had endured from men.

As they each worked to make more shifts in their energy and their behavior, things started to change. Jennifer had fun touching Steve, and he felt the joy of being desired. They were still prone to getting caught up in their busy lives and losing this newer balance—Steve would still push too hard sexually, and Jennifer would still forget how much she enjoyed sex—but they had more tools for identifying the issues and getting back on track. Jennifer did get to where it was okay with her for Steve to initiate sex, but in general, things worked better if he slowed down and gave her more room to initiate and respond. Steve learned that Jennifer needed three times the amount of foreplay that he did and that communication was part of foreplay.

Steve and Jennifer illustrate that when the high desire person stops pushing their desire, it gives their partner room to find their own innate desire instead of reacting or resisting. When given room, whatever desire they do possess can more easily come out. It's the same principle referred to as playing "hard to get." When we let go or play hard to get, it creates space for the other person to come forward. The opposite is also true. If the person with lower desire finds, and comes forward with, more desire, it frees the person with higher desire from expressing desire so frequently. Being approached and desired puts them in the receptive role, and they can more easily let go of being the initiator.

With heterosexual couples, this power struggle often looks like the woman saying, "You never touch me non-sexually; if you would touch me non-sexually then I would want to make love." The man in this situation would be feeling the opposite. "If you would touch me sexually, I would be able to relax and feel more love, and it would be easier to touch you non-sexually."

David Schnarch, in his sexual and marital therapy model, expresses this dynamic as one in which the person with the least desire controls the relationship. This applies to all aspects of a relationship. With sex, it means that if one person wants to make love and the other person doesn't, sex will not occur, and it is the person who doesn't want to make love who has control. With money, it means that if one person wants to buy something and the other person doesn't, a couple is less likely to make the purchase. The low desire person therefore controls the decision whether or not to make the purchase.

It is important for both parties in a relationship to let go of their position and move toward the needs of the other. In Schnarch's model, relationships only separate when someone makes a miscalculation and decides that they can continue to control the relationship the way they want it, without shifting to incorporate the changes their partner is seeking. Schnarch also jokingly but seriously says that the statement, "I want to work on the relationship" usually means that "I want to pound you back into the shape you were in previously."

If one person holds a lot of control in a relationship and their partner is asking for change, they may request changes of their own in an attempt to maintain the status quo, when what is really called for is for the controller to realize that they already hold control of the key areas of discourse. It is scary when our partner asks for change, and it is scary to ask for change. We all tend to remain in the status quo because we fear that our partner will abandon us if we ask for more.

If we feel that our partner holds the control of something that we desire, it is important to ask for what we want and work to feel worthy of receiving it. It could even be fair to express our needs without concern about where we will receive them. Saying that we want to have sex twice a week, and that we would prefer it to be with our mate, is the ultimate ultimatum. This would sound harsh coming from someone who already held a dominant position, but coming from someone who lacked power it might sound like a fair shift in the relationship. If a subservient partner took this "shape" or position, their partner would have to confront whether they would like to remain in control or would rather make the changes needed to keep the relationship.

Determining who controls the relationship can be simple. Just ask yourself who has the least desire for sex, who has the least desire to spend money, and the least desire for other miscellaneous things like friendships, travel, or cultural events. Sex and money are usually the two biggest areas of human need and are the main two areas where control issues can be observed. You will probably notice that the person who wants the least in these areas controls the relationship in general. Don't be too distracted by practical reality—like not having the money for a purchase or a vacation. While it might not be appropriate to spend the money, if one person is more adamant about it, it is probably a sign of this kind of control issue. It is also common for one person to control sex and the other to control money. If this is the case, both people need to work on both sides of this issue. This would entail speaking up in one area, and listening and surrendering control in another.

Control issues are usually based on fear. People tend to seek control to protect themselves from loss or abandonment. If one person is in control of the majority of the relationship's discourse, I encourage them to work deeply with their fear of loss and surrender it. If they don't address their fears, the relationship will be more likely to end, as the other person breaks free of constraint and starts to feel that they deserve to receive what they want and need. Also, it helps if we try to identify with how painful it is to live without the sex, financial habits, or leisure activities our partner desires.

We need to empathize with our partner's needs and work to get aligned with them. This was an aspect of the work that Steve and Jennifer did. Steve worked to give Jennifer the non-sexual attention she needed, but Jennifer also worked on her sexual issues and found more desire for sex. In doing so, they met in the middle and gave up their power struggle. This was a courageous act, especially for Jennifer because her lower sexual desire left her in control of sex. Because she was already getting what she wanted in their sex life (less sex), she had to empathize with Steve's need for more sex and join him in that. If they were unable to do this and meet each other half way, they may have ended their relationship.

It is helpful to realize that the high desire person is continually giving the other control by expressing needs and desires. In the area of sex, the higher desire person is giving the other control if they are always pursuing. As Steve got better at self-soothing, he took his power back. By self-soothing, he was holding his power on the inside instead of just handing it to Jennifer. Jennifer was also probably unconsciously enjoying being in control by saying no. Having Steve want her more than she wanted him kept her secure and in control because it was always clear that he wanted and desired her. His desiring her kept any of her own fears of abandonment at a safe distance.

Mutual desire is accomplished when there is an equal flow between the partners. It is important for both partners to initiate sex somewhat equally. If one person tends to do most of the initiation, it indicates that the non-initiator probably controls sex. Once this polarization is in place, both partners have a great deal of work to do to break the pattern. Both people need to move away from their position and habits and embrace and incorporate the other's perspective.

The solution, from the perspective of the person who has the most desire, is to let go of expecting or hoping for their desires to be met and become better at receiving love without sex. For many men, sex is the easiest way for them to receive love. This was the case with Steve; being wanted sexually was extremely validating, and sex helped him feel appreciated and nourished. He needed to learn additional ways to let the tenderness of love in. Steve learned to be held non-sexually, and he got better at self-soothing, which helped him let go of using sex to sooth himself. For Jennifer, the person who held less desire, the solution was to find her desire and have the strength to express it for herself, because deep down she also wanted more passion in her life.

If Steve and Jennifer were unable to create some equality in the desire patterns, Steve would have been destined to a future of painful celibate monogamy, while Jennifer would have continued to feel like a sex object. High and low desire patterns cause a polarization that goes beyond sex and creates anger and withdrawal issues in many areas. The conflict and distance may have motivated both Steve and Jennifer to have an affair—Steve driven by sex, Jennifer by needing unconditional love and non-sexual intimacy.

CHAPTER 16
RESOLVING INDUCTION PATTERNS

There are many relationship issues that result in our having a negative reaction to others' desires. If we feel pressured or induced, it is somewhat natural for us to resist others or at least feel ambivalent and disconnected from our own desires. Ambivalence or resistance can be about rebelling from authority, but the term induction helps expose the pre and peri-natal component of this. The birthing process is the earliest environment where we may have felt forced by our parents, and the obstetrician is perhaps the first authority figure we encountered. Viewing rebellion as part of an induction also helps us scrutinize the position of authority figures or partners.

Sometimes others are too invested in getting us to do something, and the investment leads to controlling behavior. It may be appropriate for us to resist until their investment and control issues are resolved. If we feel induced, it implies that we are reacting to someone, but it also begins to indicate that they may have an investment that triggers our resistance. Feeling forced leaves us in a reactive and resistant mode, which can prevent us from sharing in the risk of expressing desire for the relationship.

The most serious induction patterns usually stem from a birth experience where the baby was forced by the obstetrician to come out; however, the general issue of having parental authorities force us to do things is almost universal. In an induction pattern, we develop the habit of resisting others' advances whether they are advancing with positive or negative energy.

In childbirth, there is a general investment in getting us out of the womb safely. Almost everyone has some level of induction patterns as a result, but there are also a host of complications, which result in the obstetrician forcing us out. An induced birth is the most basic; it is when the mother is given the synthetic hormone petocin to replace the mother's naturally occurring oxytocin, which causes the uterus to contract and push the baby out. In a normal delivery, the baby secretes a hormone also, and many people hypothesize that the purpose of this may be to trigger the mother's oxytocin and initiate labor. There are other interventions, which are common at birth, which also have a similar dynamic. One is the use of forceps, which is like having your head pulled out by salad tongs, or in recent years, sucked out by a toilet plunger; another is caesarean delivery, which is being pulled out surgically.

There are a variety of reasons why the baby might not start labor—ranging from their feeling unwanted to their not feeling ready. If the family and doctor are impatient or if waiting becomes dangerous, then inducing birth with the chemical version of the mother's hormone is common. In my practice, I have found this to result in the baby feeling robbed of its choice, and it can lead to a lifelong pattern of resisting outside influence. I have often joked about people with induction issues rejecting all advances from others. It is as if you could offer them a million dollars, and they would respond, "You can't make me."

Free choice is the opposite of induction. Choosing freely because we want something instead of reacting to others' expectations is a key to resolving induction patterns. The person who feels induced will benefit from learning to choose freely, and the person who is invested or pushing (consciously or unconsciously) will benefit from letting go and giving the other space. The person who feels induced needs the affirmations:

"I choose to be here."

"People support me in the ways I like."

The person who is in the role of "the obstetrician" needs to let go of their control issues and self-soothe. Their affirmation would be:

"It is safe to surrender control."

The control issues can originate from many issues, and affirmations similar to *"I proved my way is good enough, I can relax and surrender control now,"* may be helpful.

To resolve the negative impacts of these induction interventions, it is also necessary to look at the babies' ambivalence about coming out, which may have preceded any intervention. In most cases, it is as I said above: there are deeper issues of feeling unwanted, and the induction pattern is secondary. This leads to additional affirmations, such as:

"Since I am wanted, I choose to be here, and it is safe to come out."

Although many people feel obstetricians overuse the methods of induction, forceps, and caesarean delivery, they are valuable and sometimes essential to the health and safety of the mother and baby. It is not my intent to criticize their use, but in this case to note that induction gives the baby a difficult start with authority figures and with other people's desire or advances in general.

How does an induction pattern make monogamy difficult? It results in people resisting relationships in the first place. People who were induced will tend to avoid being close to others because they fear that others will control them. Once in a relationship, it contributes to power struggles because they will avoid or rebel against their partner's influence or desires. If their partner wants a long-term relationship or monogamy, they will unconsciously rebel even if part of them wants the same thing. They will resist their partner's choice of food, movies, vacations, savings plans, friendships, and sex.

Induction patterns can be an aspect of how couples often polarize into roles, where one carries the desire and the other carries the indifference. The person with the desire is perceived as trying to induce or force the other into doing something they don't want to do. This impacts intimacy even if both partners essentially want it. The induced or low desire partner will resist intimacy if the other initiates it, even if they generally want it in the first place.

This whole pattern is different from situations where we do not want someone or are not attracted to them in the first place. If we are only interested in some aspects of a relationship, then it is appropriate to have boundaries and limits that define our level of desire. If we don't want to date someone, it makes sense that we would resist his or her advances. If we want a divorce, it is understandable that we resist our partner. If we have a predominant lifelong pattern of resisting relationships and generally having low desire for anyone, then it would be helpful to look at this issue.

There is another side to this pattern. If we are expressing desire, it can put us in the role of the parent or obstetrician, and others may feel pressured or suffocated by us. If this is the case, we will benefit from working with our own authority and control issues. People who initiate are trying to control, too. An additional term breathworker's use to express both sides of these induction patterns is the "obstetrician syndrome." The obstetrician syndrome is about how the obstetrician's investment in our birth resulted in them often controlling it and not allowing our mothers or us to do it our way. This results in the mother and/or child feeling invalidated and controlled by the outside influence of the obstetrician and leads to rebellion. The obstetrician syndrome refers to both sides of this issue. First, the rebellion to which I already referred, where we will tend to resist if a friend or authority approaches us with investment or the desire to control us, or the outcome of the relationship.

Secondly, if we express strong desire, opinions, or authority, we will be more likely to trigger someone's resistance or rebellion. For one person to be in the rebellious role of resisting, the other person has to be in the role of the obstetrician who is trying to control the outcome. All relationship dynamics can be released from either end. If we are in the role of the obstetrician in our relationship, by trying to get our partner to want us, or do more of what we want to do, we need to surrender the parental authority and find our own softer, shyer, submissive, or receptive side. In short, extroverted or authoritative people are the basic opposites of people who hold back because of induction patterns. People with strong authority or extroversion will also naturally push people into resistance.

My use of the word control is not intended to be as judgmental as it may sound. Control issues are part of some seriously negative and abusive relationship issues, but the term control also helps us identify the natural and somewhat inevitable process of seeking love, security, or safety in the world. When we feel insecure, we are more likely to push to gain love and thus end up in the role of the obstetrician. This does not necessarily mean that we are a controlling abuser. It is helpful for everyone to get comfortable identifying their need to control situations so we can get the love we need. Doing so usually does not take the extreme proportions that we often associate with the term control.

Again, this is much the same as other descriptions of parental dynamics. To be in the role of the obstetrician is to be in a parental role, and to be feeling induced is similar to feeling like a rebellious child. While these ideas are similar to others often expressed when we talk about rebelling against authority, it is my feeling that the awareness of the patterns deepen if we realize that authority issues are often shaped by our birth experience and the obstetrician syndrome, as well as by experiences with parents and other authorities.

CHAPTER 17
PURSUING A RELATIONSHIP

Another common way couples tend to have different desire patterns is in the area of wanting their relationship. These same principles are central to what happens when a couple is dating, deciding to live together or to marry, as well as the partnership issues like sex and money addressed above. It is common for one person to want the relationship more than the other, and that can lead to a polarization where a couple can get stuck in the roles in which one is pursuing and the other is resisting or ambivalent.

My ex-wife Paula and I were no exception to this, and during the first few months we were together, I had the most desire to get married. We had set a date for our wedding, but Paula expressed some uncertainty about whether or not this was the right thing to do. This forced me to let go, self-soothe, and do some more internal work about my worthiness and self-esteem as she resolved her issues. After a short period, she resolved a majority of her doubts, and once she did, my own doubts surfaced and I had to examine them.

This kind of flux in desires is very common. When one person is carrying a large percentage of a particular energy, the other will be likely to carry the opposite energy. If one person is pushing the desire for the relationship, the other will express the doubt. I have seen this with many couples. This was the case with Marcia and Charles, a young couple with whom I worked recently. Marcia was ready to get married and have a family, and she was certain that she wanted to do this with Charles. Charles was in love with Marcia, too, but was less eager to "settle down." He was concerned that he might not be ready to commit to marriage and children.

Marcia and Charles had polarized into the roles where Marcia had more desire and was chasing Charles; Charles was feeling the lower desire of the induced role. Marcia had entered into a kind of chasing mode and couldn't even feel her own doubt because she was so busy chasing Charles to secure his love. More importantly, her chasing was pushing Charles further into doubt. This brought the focus of the relationship to Charles until his doubts were resolved.

We worked with these principles and Marcia backed off, self-soothed, and worked to feel worthy of love and marriage regardless of whether Charles wanted to marry her. Charles worked to feel secure enough within himself to express his love and commitment to Marcia and let go of reacting to feeling pressured. Once Charles did this and embraced his desire for Marcia, it made it easier for her to let go of chasing, face her own uncertainties, and resolve her own doubts. It certainly helps anyone resolve their doubts if the person with whom they are in a relationship stops chasing and works internally to self-soothe and maintain self-esteem.

This can also be explained conversely from Charles' point of view. He was so busy fielding Marcia's desires that he tended to forget the part of him that desired her. Marcia's desire had pushed him metaphorically (and literally) back onto his heels, and he had become doubtful and numb to his desire. To work his way out of this he needed to resolve his own issues around being pressured or induced. By resolving them, he was able to stop reacting to Marcia, and his natural love for her was able to come out. He was able to come out (stop running) and give himself room to find his own desire.

People tend to become polarized in chaser and chasee roles, and the key to shifting this dynamic is to work with the issues that make you chase to get love or those that make you resist love. If one person works on their side of this equation, the relationship dynamics will shift, and it becomes easier for the other person to then resolve their issues and find their sense of security and desire for the relationship. Shifting these dynamics also gives both people the ability to see the relationship more clearly.

CHAPTER 18
CHRONICLE #4: SEXUALITY AND SEXUAL ATTRACTIONS

The heterosexual stereotype of the man having greater sexual desire has only been partly applicable in my life. I have had partners who wanted sexual intimacy as frequently as I did. I have also had some major relationships where the desire patterns polarized, and I wanted more sexual intimacy than my partner did. This was the case with Paula and me. Throughout our entire relationship, I tended to hold the most sexual desire, and we suffered from being polarized into a high and low desire pattern. While we enjoyed good sex, we weren't aligned about the frequency of sex even at the very beginning of our relationship. Although I was frequently upset that we did not make love very often, my love for Paula always transcended this. In hindsight, I see that my attempts to discuss and resolve this were too few.

Frequently the best solution to differences in how often sex is desired is to create more connection and communication, which naturally results in more sex within the relationship. Developing tools for accepting sexual differences while maintaining monogamy is also an important step. It is especially important for a person in the high desire position to have a model for how to deal with their attraction to others.

I am fond of saying, "You're supposed to be attracted to attractive people," and "Most people are more beautiful than they are ugly." This means that I find most people attractive, and being heterosexual, I find most women to be sexually attractive. This kind of general attraction has never posed any significant problems for me. What I find to be significant is how we handle it when we meet someone to whom we're *really* attracted.

I would say that I have met an average of one person per year to whom I was really attracted. I don't just mean physical attraction. I mean physically, emotionally, and spiritually—someone who I would imagine to be a suitable life partner. At the beginning of my relationship with Paula, I would maintain my monogamous connection and my sanity by running away from these people. In addition, I would generally avoid connecting with all attractive women. After about five years of this, I decided to lighten up about this issue and practice what I preached about all of my feelings being valid and sexual attractions being normal. I also knew, and taught, that you could learn a lot about yourself by examining your feelings of attraction (and repulsion). I changed my strategy and began to move toward the women to whom I was attracted in order to explore these emotions. My ability to make this change was also a result of my feeling more secure in my ability to remain monogamous.

It is hard to describe exactly how I created this security. As I grew in life and worked to resolve each issue from abandonment to self-esteem, I became more secure and less driven by my sexuality. I laugh as I write this because I am still plenty driven by my sexuality. But with this increased security, I no longer needed the rigid boundary I maintained by staying away from women. Understanding the distinction between feelings and behavior helped me maintain a strong intention not to have an affair but to allow and accept all of my sexual feelings.

Initially, my attractions might take the form of strong sexual fantasy, which might include fantasizing about how wonderful it would be to have a sexual relationship. I call part of what happens in these early relationship fantasies the fantasy bond. The fantasy bond is the tendency to fantasize that a person (or place, organization, career, community, etc.) is more ideal than they actually are. The driving force behind this is the need to feel that you are loved and secure, and will be successful. The ultimate fantasy bond is with our parents— we need to feel that they are doing a good job protecting us in the world, so we tend to fantasize that they are better parents than they actually are.

I have found it to be healing to remain in contact and not avoid people to whom I have a strong attraction. By doing this, I have greater opportunity to work through my fantasy bonds and see the object of my attraction more objectively for who they really are. In the end, this gives me the ability to feel and embrace my own yearnings within myself and let go of longing for a fix from the outside world. It also takes the fire off of the attraction.

When I was with Paula, if I were to have continually avoided my attractions, I would have been more likely to avoid my feelings, particularly those about lacking love and intimacy in my life or our relationship. By being present with my feelings, and letting them evolve through the fantasy and reach a point where the person I found attractive became just another ordinary person, I was then faced with my feelings about myself and my life without the illusion that the object of my attraction would save me. This is very practical because not only did it more clearly force me to do my own inner work, but it also forced me to directly confront my feelings about what was lacking in my primary relationship.

It is rare that I feel the need to discuss my attractions with anyone. I consider talking about attractions to be optional, and the pros and cons of discussing attractions are very personal. In general, I subscribe to the notion that the truth always heals. Discussing an issue is much healthier than hiding it, and expressing your feelings will help dissipate some of the intensity surrounding them. However, people are, in general, very phobic about sexuality. It is a deep trigger for vulnerable feelings or the fear of abandonment. An important first step is to get to know how your partner feels about this. I have dated women who found men's voyeuristic tendencies to "girl watch" to be very offensive. In this case, I moved as gently as possible but also sought to tell the truth and get the issue out into the open. It is helpful if both parties in a relationship are able to talk about people they find attractive.

Only discuss your attractions to the degree that you need to in order to facilitate letting go of them. This is a highly personal point, and I would not recommend that you use this point to justify staying closeted about your attractions. If you avoid talking about this, it will cause problems because if the attraction becomes disowned it will gain strength. You will not necessarily notice this consciously, but the attractions and the yearnings will be there. The majority of couples live with this unspoken, and it sits in the emotional space of the relationship like an elephant in the living room (or should I say bedroom).

One way I have communicated about my attractions was to make it clear in a gentle way that I had a tendency to find women attractive in general. I share this without specifically mentioning a particular individual or situation. This creates an opening so that the issue is not closeted or stuck. Because it is shared in a general way, it is less likely to trigger my partner's abandonment issues, or make a person to whom I am attracted unnecessarily uncomfortable.

Another fairly typical aspect of my sexual attractions is that I have never had a close relationship with a woman without being able to imagine that it would be enjoyable to make love with her. This means that I might have a close friend to whom I was not attracted initially, but as the friendship developed, it would either pass through a phase of accepting and integrating sexual feelings or occasionally having a fleeting sexual attraction. This kind of attraction often occurred with my partner's friends, or with couples with whom we became close. Accepting and not avoiding these feelings is a critical aspect of developing real, non-sexual friendship. If I were to have suppressed these feelings, it would likely lead to some sort of avoidance or distance in the relationship.

The suppression of sexual attraction is sometimes a part of why people dislike each other. I had a friend who seemed to have difficulty maintaining his monogamy and was highly critical of many of his wife's female friends. I noticed that many of these friends were very attractive. Later, when he had an affair with one of them, I felt that his tendency to criticize was an attempt to distance himself from his attractions. Fighting or criticizing can serve to buffer us from our attraction and keep us safe. We can tune into this further by observing a similar dynamic between parents and adolescent children. The adult picks fights with the adolescent as a means of keeping a safe distance and staying away from incestuous feelings. I certainly recommend this distance over acting out incest, but the distance is unnecessary. Parents can learn to accept their unconscious sexual feelings and move beyond them into real intimacy, just as an adult can with another adult. It is the same as with any other feeling: when experienced and accepted, feelings transform. In the case of parents and children, the intimacy that remains will not be sexual at all. This, of course, applies only to parents who are not pedophiles, which is the vast majority.

Before I continue, I want to describe the importance of embracing attractions and sexual feelings in another way. *Sexual feelings* are innocent and inevitable and should be distinguished from behavior. Our behavior is not always innocent, but the essence of our feelings is. If we do not admit to our feelings of attraction to others, the suppression will be more likely to lead to our becoming obsessed with sex and sexuality. These obsessions are more likely to lead to behaviors that cause ourselves and others pain. If we preach "hellfire and brimstone," we are more likely to become entrenched in it. In psychology, this dynamic has often been called repression/obsession dualism, which means that when we repress a feeling we are more likely to become obsessed with it. I find this to be the best explanation of why we often hear of corrupt morals coming from the highest of places. It often requires a lot of repression to push ourselves to higher values.

When we repress our feelings, they get pushed into our

subconscious, where they grow stronger. The energy we spend pushing them down gives them added validity and they gain strength. The image of a volcano best describes this. Our feelings have a natural flow to them. In the area of sexuality, if we have a body with strong life energy, we will have strong sexual/erotic feelings. If we repress them, it's like putting a lid on a volcano. They will be less likely to erupt violently if we release the pressure behind them a little bit at a time by acknowledging their existence.

It is also helpful to realize that our sexual desires are not always based on sex. Our society is training people, especially men, to use sex as an outlet for other feelings. The volcano of sexual desire is fueled by other forces, and the more comfortable we can get admitting our other needs—such as needing to be liked, appreciated, or held—the less likely we will be to transfer those needs to sex. Admitting the whole range of human needs will help us take the pressure off the volcano, too.

A key to dealing with our sexual attractions is to relax about sex. Being less worried about remaining monogamous will reduce our sense of pressure, and we will be more able to deal with what drives the volcano. My father's non-monogamy caused my family pain, and it contributed to the importance of monogamy for me. I have worked to reduce the pressure I place on this value by trying to accept that it is "just sex," and relax and not draw negative conclusions about the moral character of others who have been rumored to have had affairs. I have also relaxed by admitting that I, and others, have strong sexual feelings toward many people. By admitting that I have attractions to other women, I am less likely to be "blind sided" by a volcano of suppressed desire. By keeping my desire in my consciousness all along, I become better at dealing with inner conflicts, releasing the pressure behind sexual attractions bit by bit, and remaining conscious of my larger desire to be monogamous.

CHAPTER 19
SEXUAL FANTASY AND MASTURBATION

The topic of sexual fantasy and masturbation can be deeply upsetting. To some degree, we accept that imagining having sex with people other than our partner is normal (at least for men). But we underestimate how upsetting this can be, particularly for women, who do not have these kinds of fantasy or masturbation habits themselves. With the increase of pornography, our culture has taken this so far that it is important to look at both the natural and destructive nature of fantasy and masturbation.

Throughout my career and life leading up to the conception and writing of this book, I took the position that allowing yourself to have non-monogamous fantasies is one of the easiest ways to accept and work through attractions without acting on them. I still feel that this idea holds some value, but I am increasingly looking at both sides of this issue: Is it healthy to fantasize about having sex with people to whom you are attracted? To imagine making love with someone on whom you have a crush while you masturbate? To view pornography?

When attractions and fantasies exist, it is important not to suppress them. If we do, they will only become stronger and more volcanic. There are those who prefer "energetic" or "psychic monogamy," meaning that they feel that even one's thoughts and fantasies should be monogamous, but I don't think this is realistic. I have found that many of the people who sought to maintain "energetic monogamy" or "monogamy in thought" were the ones who became the least able to maintain monogamous relationships. We are used to seeing people of high moral ground fall from grace and have affairs, but you may find it equally powerful to hear that I have found this also to be true for less conservative people, like psychotherapists and personal growth trainers. Even in these circles where we would expect less repression/obsession dualism, I have found that those who are dogmatically opposed to non-monogamous fantasies are more likely to be having affairs.

To understand further the pro-fantasy side of this issue, it helps if we distinguish the difference between thoughts and behaviors. A few non-sexual examples will illustrate these points in a different way. If we have an angry thought, does that make us a mean person? If we imagine hitting someone, does that make us violent? Having these thoughts in our inner world is part of being a free individual. We do not have the right to hurt others by acting on them, but we are free in our minds. In working with dysfunctional family issues, one problem is that often a child's inner world of thoughts and feelings are controlled by the parents' rigidity. In a dysfunctional family, a child's feelings may be invalidated to the point where they are not allowed to have feelings of anger or dislike.

In a functional family, children are entitled to their feelings, and their feelings are distinguished from behavior. A functional family does not allow the child to be mean to others or hurt others, but the feelings are valid. If a child hates their sibling and wishes that they were dead, it does not make them a bad person. Invalidating a child's anger at a sibling will serve to exacerbate sibling rivalry at a future point.

This is the same point about repression/obsession dualism and feelings that eventually become volcanic if we suppress them. If we can accept our anger as fleeting, and not a serious statement of who we really are, then why can't we accept our sexual attractions as just feelings that don't define us? If you still have a problem with this, realize that sex and anger are among the most taboo issues in our culture. These same questions could be asked about something more mundane, such as, *Does wanting to take a nap make you lazy? Does wanting more money make you greedy? Does imagining eating two desserts mean that you don't care about your health?* Of course not, but fantasies and masturbation can still cause some problems. It can fuel shame and guilt and result in our withdrawing from our partner. It is also possible to fantasize in an addictive way that just creates a fragmented or secret life.

This topic is easier to accept for people who have fantasies and or fantasize about others while masturbating. I have found that men are more apt to fantasize with a specific person in mind than women are. The object of the fantasy may be a friend, a clerk, or a porn star. Women's fantasies and masturbation are more apt to be less visual and more feeling based. The problem with fantasy and masturbation can be expressed like this: Just because it is common for men to masturbate in a visual way, and we can explain this from a biological and anthropological perspective, does not mean that continuing this behavior supports our current relationship goals. It can be very hurtful to partners when we are not psychically monogamous. This hurt reduces true safety, intimacy, and depth of relationships, and the lack of depth perpetuates the fantasies.

Fantasies and masturbation are part of the more predatory male nature of yearning for more and more superficial sexual contact. This is an aspect of male aggression, which leaves partners feeling unsafe. This is especially difficult for heterosexual couples because it becomes a perpetual problem, where since a woman does not feel the safety she needs to be sexually intimate, the man doesn't get what he needs either. The lack of intimacy perpetuates the leaving (literally or energetically) to get his needs met. To break this cycle, men need to recover form hunting, chasing, and conquering. Women need to recover from being hurt and left. Both need to stop withholding or withdrawing from loving each other.

Connecting both sides of this issue means understanding that we cause ourselves problems if we fear or suppress our fantasies, and we cause ourselves problems if we act on them. While fantasy and masturbation are normal, they are also something from which we are recovering. They are hurtful because the vulnerable inner child does not distinguish between fantasy and reality as easily as the rational mind does. Each person needs to decide how to handle their sexual desires and how truthful to be with their partner. If you do fantasize about others when you masturbate, I recommend that you only minimally communicate about it with your partner. I don't recommend you say, "My crush on your best friend is subsiding. I think the masturbation fantasies I'm having about her are really helping." Or, "My romance novel fantasy of being carried off to the bushes by the pirate with a muscular chest is still giving me a lot of pleasure."

On the other hand, I would recommend that your partner know something about your masturbation habits. As far as fantasies or attractions in general, it helps lighten the repression issues if you have some discussion about what kind of people you find attractive. For example, which film stars do you find most interesting and attractive? Discuss this at a time when this is not a hot button for either one of you.

Although certain fantasies may be healthy, I am extremely against pornography, and I detail my reasons in a later chapter. It is also important to note that whatever level of fantasy is normal for you, you should not fantasize about people other than your partner while making love.

It is interesting to note that some sex therapists have encouraged this over the years. It is called "bypassing," and it was encouraged because it got some couples, who had lost interest and connection, to have sex. A more current tenant of sex therapy discourages this because it is contrary to true intimacy, which requires being physically and emotionally present.

Other fantasies or role-play that change some characteristics of your partner can be healthy. If you act out a fantasy where your partner is a delivery person that you just met, and you make love, it is different from bypassing because you are still making love to your partner's personality and body. In any role-play, it is important that it be your partner's body and essence that you are imagining.

There are many needs and desires we express and fulfill through our sexuality. I will be addressing these throughout the book. Our fantasies represent our needs and yearnings. The more we are conscious of those needs and seek to meet them constructively, the healthier our life and relationships will be. The more we get our needs met in our partnerships, the more intimate they will be. If we avoid what we need from our partner and direct that energy elsewhere, our relationships remain unfulfilling. The real issue here is to direct our desire to our partner.

CHAPTER 20
DREAMS AND MESSAGES

It is asking far too much for us to be monogamous in our subconscious dream life. If we felt that our dreams should be monogamous, we would be setting ourselves up for severe repression/obsession dualism. There are many good and valid approaches to dream analysis. One tendency that many approaches have in common is that they treat dreams as an outlet for our subconscious mind. Our dreams are a way that our subconscious communicates with us. Our subconscious expresses feelings through symbols in our dreams in hopes that we might become conscious of the energy or the feelings that exist in us. It doesn't mean that we want the literal interpretation of what we're dreaming. Sometimes it means we need to accept and stop resisting the feelings.

For example, it is not uncommon to have incestuous dreams, non-monogamous dreams, or for heterosexuals to have homosexual dreams and homosexuals to have heterosexual dreams. I've had sexual dreams that made me uncomfortable once I was awake. If we have an incestuous dream where we are making love to our mother, it doesn't necessarily mean that we *want* to have sex with her. It more likely means that we have suppressed sexual feelings for her, or that we want a greater connection with her or with our own inner mothering qualities. If a heterosexual has a homosexual dream or vise versa, it does not mean that we are interested in engaging in this type of sex, but that we need to relax about our homophobia and accept our sexuality on a deeper level. If a man dreams of having sex with a man, it could mean that he is connecting on a deeper level with an aspect of himself that is represented by the man in the dream.

You might imagine from my assertion that sexual fantasies are innocent that I also feel that non-monogamous dreams are innocent and serve a purpose similar to having conscious fantasies. Carl Jung called the female figure in men's dreams the anima, and defined it as their inner feminine component. For women, the parallel male figure is called the animus. In Jungian psychology, having contact with an anima or animus figure is viewed as a man's way of connecting with his inner feminine energy, and likewise, the animus is a woman's way of connecting with her inner masculine energy. Although these words can be heterocentric, the basic theory further illustrates the points I'm making. For example, a man having homosexual dreams could be about connecting with his animus, the inner masculine part of himself.

While for a man, Jung's theory means that romancing or having sex with a woman in his dreams means he is embracing his inner feminine qualities, dreams can also simply be a way for the subconscious mind to express non-monogamous desires and encourage us to deal with our yearning for more or different sexual contact. By getting these messages or dreams, we can consciously handle our

113

monogamy and confront what isn't working in our relationships. In the meantime, it is like any form of fantasy—if it is suppressed, it only builds in intensity and comes back stronger and more volcanic.

I am not advocating that we should seek to have an abundance of fantasy outlets in order to maintain our monogamy. I am saying that we need to listen to our fantasies because they are giving us information about what is lacking in our lives and ourselves. Our relationships are likely to flourish if we listen to our dreams and fantasies, use their input to confront our current situation, and let them push us toward what we need to develop. It's quite simple: If we have fantasies in conscious or subconscious form, we are seeking a connection with the "energy" about which we are fantasizing. It could be about an energy that is missing in our partnership, or it could be a part of ourselves that needs recognition and acceptance. If we are not in a primary relationship, the same principle applies—our fantasies help us connect with our desire for connection, nurturing, eroticism, and belonging. By embracing our desires, we are more able to fulfill them, whether from within ourselves or in relationship with another.

There are a wide variety of human needs that we seek to achieve through sexual fantasies and sexual contact. If we use our fantasies and dreams consciously, we can guide ourselves toward creating more sex and connection in our primary relationship.

CHAPTER 21
SEXUAL AND RELATIONAL ADDICTIONS

It is important to balance this book's pro-sexuality perspective with a discussion of sexual addiction. To a sex addict, this book could be just another excuse to allow patterns of sexual addiction to continue. With behavior addictions like food, gambling, shopping, and sex, I apply the phrase, "It is not what you do, it is how you do it that counts." Sex is healthy. Eating and shopping are healthy; however, we can do these things in a way that is unhealthy, obsessive, compulsive, destructive, or designed to avoid deeper issues.

In the mainstream view of addiction, a key aspect of what defines a behavior or substance as an addiction is the point where it is destructive to our health or relationships. For example, with alcohol, if we drink to a point where it negatively affects our health, work, or relationships then we benefit from viewing this as an addiction and from seeking treatment and sobriety. Many people apply a pretty severe standard to describe a negative effect and usually only label themselves or a friend as an alcoholic if the effects of alcohol are quite destructive—for example if their drinking leads to a loss of job or relationship, or creates a serious health problem.

I prefer to use a broader and more "holistic" definition of addiction in my work, which defines addiction as "the habit of not feeling" or "the ways we avoid feeling." While it can be applied to substance and behavioral addictions that recovery communities address, this definition expands our notion of addiction into a "process," which includes virtually everyone and every activity to a degree. We all have behaviors or habits that we use to avoid or "fix" our feelings. We might not use drugs, food, sex, gambling, shopping, television, or exercising in a way that is destructive, but we will still benefit from looking at what, if any, feelings we may be avoiding by engaging in these activities. In this model, thinking is the ultimate addiction. We can even think as a way of not being present or in order to avoid what we are feeling.

Again I want to repeat the phrase, "It's not what you do, it is how you do it." Clearly, thinking is normal. So are sex and a moderate amount of television. However, there can be a process of avoidance that is a core problem that needs to be addressed. The process of healing addiction and creating successful relationships is about "learning to feel again," meaning it involves undoing the habits of avoidance and replacing them with being present emotionally. I recommend a variety of tools and processes in addition to voice dialogue and breathwork that enable people to learn to feel more fully. The common components of these processes are learning to express emotion and to identify and express what we feel. Ultimately letting go of addiction is a moment-to-moment process of learning to be present instead of using activity or substances to avoid feeling. To heal addiction is to become a "human being" instead of a "human doing."

This holistic view of addiction can be understood further if we view our behavior as "musical addiction." Inspired by the game of musical chairs, musical addiction is my term to describe that while we may not do any one thing in excess, we may rotate from one substance or activity to another in a way that produces an avoidance of feeling. We might come home from work, have a snack, then process some mail, watch television, exercise, call a friend, watch more television, eat dinner, read, masturbate, do some housework, talk to another friend, have another snack, and watch some more television. All of these activities are fine and healthy in themselves, but if we are using them to avoid our feelings, we could benefit from seeing them as part of an addictive process. Note that even activities as healthy as reading and exercise can be done to avoid feelings, and can therefore be addictions.

If we view addiction as a process like this, then if we find ourselves opening the door of the refrigerator when we aren't really hungry, we can ask ourselves what we are feeling. We can also skip an activity, sit still for a moment, and ask ourselves what we are feeling. For example, masturbation is a healthy thing; but I also recommend that if you masturbate regularly, on occasion, instead just experience your feelings without masturbating. Applying this approach to sex means that our addictive process might take two forms: first, a more destructive pattern, where our use of sex, masturbation, or pornography is interfering more noticeably with our life and relationships; second, where sex is part of our "musical addiction," and we use sex, masturbation, or pornography to act out unresolved issues or avoid feelings.

I view the process of healing addiction as learning to be present while we are being or doing anything, and the biggest key to succeeding at being present is our overall personal growth. The more resolved we are with all potential life or relationship issues, the more present we will be. If we are actively engaged in our therapy process and begin to look at our behaviors more consciously, we will be reversing the addictive process and creating our life as a recovery process. Life and activity can be lived more consciously, and as such be like meditating—learning to feel and be present.

I also feel it is valuable to stick to the basics and view the first step in healing addiction as letting go of serious destructive addictions. For most people, that will probably mean complete abstinence from the substance(s) or behavior(s) all together. It is easy to see how substance addictions that numb our body and feelings by creating altered states do not support our emotional and physical health. If we have an issue with a substance, or substances, then addressing it specifically is certainly more important than working with my musical addiction model. By letting go of the addiction, the feelings we were avoiding or fixing can then come to the surface and be healed. Often this is a life-long process.

If behavioral addictions like gambling, shopping, overeating, sex, or pornography have reached destructive proportions and are eroding life or relationships, it is equally important to seek intervention, treatment, and recovery. Some of these addictions, such as gambling or pornography, can be eliminated completely, whereas addictions to food, sex, and shopping probably require that we seek a healthy balance. Here breaking the cycle of addiction will usually require a period of abstinence followed by reintroducing the behavior in a way that is healthy.

Ultimately, it is up to us to admit and face our own issues and problems. If our friends and loved ones feel we are an addict, they can share their feelings about it, but it is up to us to make changes. I feel very strongly about the notion that "you're an addict when you say you are." The idea that our own admission is key may apply more to addiction than to any other life issue. Sometimes others intervene, but the key to change is our acceptance and admission of our problems. We are the one who has to get out of denial. Sometimes we will feel we have a problem when others don't think we do. If one drink makes us feel bad, we might want to call ourselves an alcoholic. If we feel that our moderate use of pornography is negatively affecting real intimacy, we might want to label it a pornography addiction and not worry about how it fits within a destructive or holistic model.

It also helps to realize that people with active addictions are not going to encourage us to see our addictions as problems. With something like pornography, which we know to be potentially dangerous, I would recommend that we listen more to those who have faced these issues than those who are trying to use it, even in a moderate way.

It is helpful to expand the notion of sexual addiction and include it in a broader model of "Relational Addiction." For many people, an issue similar to sex addiction exists in the area of love and relationships. In this model, the relational addictions are viewed as sex, relationships, and fantasy/romance. A sex addiction is when the "fix" is obtained through the act of sex. A relationship addiction would be where the "fix" lies in the idea of being in a relationship. A fantasy or romance addiction is where the "fix" is obtained through the fantasies or images of love or romance. The broader issue is that there are various ways we can seek love and connection. It is possible that our seeking love and connection can become an addiction when we use it to fix or compensate for unresolved feelings, usually related to feelings of low self-worth.

Understanding the difference between sex, relationship, and fantasy/romance addictions is helpful because we may favor one method of compensating over the others. To the sex addict, the drive to feel worthy takes the form of desiring sex, and the fix is in the act of sex. They unconsciously feel as if the high of sex and sexual connection makes them feel worthy. It is as if the sex addict feels "if he/she wanted me sexually, then I would feel better and feel like a more worthy person."

To the relationship addict, it is the idea of being loved and in a relationship that provides the fix. The relationship addict feels that "if he/she wanted me then I would feel better." And, to the fantasy or romance addict it is the images of love and connection that provide the fix. They unconsciously feel that "if we could have a candlelight dinner and walk on the beach together, then I would feel better."

The trouble with relationship addiction is that the need to be in a relationship can be a cover up for feelings of personal lack. While the drive for an intimate primary relationship is also normal and healthy, it is important to discuss it as an addiction because it can reach destructive levels and have negative consequences. In the holistic model, it can be a way we avoid feelings of low self-esteem.

The questions to ask are these: Are we neglecting other aspects of our lives to create relationships? Are we spending money we don't have? Are we neglecting our work or children to create relationships? Basically, if we are coming from a dependant or obsessive place, it is important to develop our independent side and the ability to self-soothe.

Fantasy or romance addiction is less talked about than sex and relationship addiction, but it is interesting to note that it is possible for one's weak link to be in this area. Here the "fix" is in the images of love and relationship. It is valuable to realize that images or rituals like candlelight dinners, moonlit nights, beach vacations, and cuddling by the fire are not necessarily intimate in themselves. A fantasy addict is attached to them but is not actually present in their body or the relationship. This can be destructive just as with sex and relationship addiction if the need for the fix increases and takes on expensive or time-consuming proportions.

A fantasy addict also tends to seek but not find a relationship. They go through life looking, even praying for a relationship, but since the attachment and habit is to the images of love, reality will tend to fall short of their fantasies, and they will become discouraged after the honeymoon phase of a relationship passes.

Sex, relationship, and fantasy/romance addictions are a source of non-monogamous tendencies where someone seeks new lovers because it provides a stimulus that real life and relationships do not. In the area of love and relationships, it is best to give up the "hunt" and settle into accepting current relationships.

Discussing the possibility that sex and relationships can be addictions is complicated because the desires for sex, love, and relationships are also healthy. They are human needs and should be accepted as part of the need to belong. On the other hand, they can also be used to avoid deeper issues and other needs. I have said much about how the inability to be intimate or in a relationship is a problem. I do not intend to make the reader fear that our desires are addictive; instead, I want to point out that there are two sides to the issue. While embracing our desires and seeking intimacy is healthy, we can take our desires too far and seek connection in a compulsive or obsessive way.

Whether we apply a destructive model or a holistic model, we all need to become aware of what our weakest link may be in the area of relational addiction. Even when it doesn't take destructive form, I find that most of us have a weakness in the way we seek love. By understanding whether we tend toward sex, relationship, or fantasy/romance addiction, we can better work with the issues underneath our desires. While we may not have a behavior in its destructive form, we may have it as part of our musical addiction and use it as a means to execute the habit of not feeling.

The Trouble with Sex Addiction and Pornography

It is important to have an understanding of how sexual desire can go too far and become part of a destructive pattern that should be treated like any other addiction. One should certainly be concerned if sex is the main or only way that one seeks intimate contact with a partner. In its destructive form, a sex addict may consciously want to choose a long period of celibacy in order to begin healing the addiction. In the musical addiction model, if someone has a relationship where they have a lot of sex, they should consider replacing sex with other contact more often. Having dinner and talking could actually be more intimate.

Whether one is in a relationship or single, masturbation is a common form of sex addiction. There is a wide range of what might be considered a healthy amount of masturbation. Some people may masturbate fourteen times a week and still consider it healthy. A good way to evaluate any addiction's destructive tendency is to see if it is replacing intimacy with others or interfering with regular activities like work, homemaking, or parenting. If someone is masturbating instead of making love with his or her partner, or if one is interrupting work to masturbate, it is a problem. If someone felt they had a masturbation problem that was destructive, I would suggest they seek near complete abstinence for a time. In general, I recommend that almost everyone work to become free of the addictive tendency to masturbate by regularly choosing not to masturbate and see what feelings surface.

Pornography is a form of sexual addiction that can be quite troublesome. It is clear that men use pornography more often than women do, and this is in part because they have a tendency to have more specific visual fantasies. While pornography is not always destructive, it seems that with the invention of the Internet, as well as the increase of graphic sexual content in our media and movies, the use of pornography is becoming increasingly problematic.

This is a good place to make the very basic point that addictions escalate because we become desensitized to stimulus. We become desensitized by using something to avoid feelings. The more we use that thing, the more of it we are likely to need in order to accomplish the suppression. Stimulus becomes a method of distraction from unresolved feelings. Stimulus also acts as a positive reward by taking us to good feelings, which helps us avoid pain. The more we do this, the more stimulus we are likely to need to accomplish the distraction or the suppression of the unconscious feelings. Just as a heavy drinker develops a tolerance to alcohol and needs more to provide the mood change, so, too, does the sex addict. Truly what begins as a fascination with pornography (or anything) can become an obsession where more and more of the fix is needed to create the high. In the case of pornography, this can be both expensive and drain large amounts of time from real relationships and intimacy. Even worse, it can desensitize someone so that they are no longer aroused by intimate face-to-face sexual contact.

Desensitization is a key word here with any addiction. Addictions grow because the initial dose of the drug or behavior becomes inadequate to provide the high. In the case of pornography, something that is initially arousing, such as pictures of naked women or men, can lead to the addict needing other extremes, such as violence, bestiality, or pedophilia to create a stimulus similar to what the picture of the naked woman once provided. Extreme sexual images have little to do with intimacy and are less likely to be mutually enjoyed or created as part of an intimate sex life.

Even if pornographic images are not extreme, they do create unrealistic images of what good sexual relationships are. The porn star can become the norm of what a man wants in order to be fulfilled. An average man with an average body would be better served to be attracted to an average woman with an average body. If porn makes us accustomed to unrealistic images then it will inhibit us from being satisfied with reality. Pornography can then replace relationships.

There are people in this world neglecting their children so they can view pornography. According to www.mykidsbrowser.com, the pornography industry grosses $57 billion per year worldwide—$12 billion in the United States. There are 4.2 million pornographic web sites and 2.5 billion pornographic emails per day. This is 8% of all email. That's a lot of people spending a lot of time on pornography. It is not just a male issue either. According to www.wisechoice.net, 72% of men and 28% of women visit porn sites.

While I believe pornography is a negative thing, complete abstinence from it may not be necessary for everyone. I also believe strongly in my earlier discussion of repression/obsession dualism—that if we repress things completely, we will more likely create obsessions. We don't need to make pornography forbidden fruit. We can look at it consciously, and even discuss it with our teenage children, in a way that helps let go of sex taboos and teaches why it is best to limit it and not view it regularly.

Sexual Avoidance

It is also valuable to note that most models that address, sex, relationships, and fantasy/romance addiction also include the tendency to avoid sex or relationships as an addictive pattern. We can become addicted to avoiding sex and intimacy. Here some theorists have even used the term "sexual anorexia" to describe this. While this book's pro-sexuality perspective has already addressed this in a general way, I mention this here just to complete the basic vocabulary that is part of working with sex and relational addiction.

Sexual avoidance could involve staying away from any contact that could lead to flirting; flirting but then not accepting an invitation for a date; or having a relationship but making sure to avoid sex. Someone who is in a relationship may make sure their partner doesn't see them nude to reduce the chances of being approached sexually. They may go to bed late or at a different time from their partner, or generally remain too busy to have the time or energy for sex. People who are sexually avoidant may even tend to dislike sexual humor and sexual movies, as if they were a threat to their abstinence.

Resolving sexual avoidance requires a similar but opposite approach to resolving sexual addiction. Just as the sex addict needs to obtain and then confront the feelings underneath the behavior, the person who is sexually avoidant would stop avoiding sex and sexuality and address their feelings. It is important to begin to address the feelings before pushing yourself into a more sexual arena. Counseling is always helpful and makes a lot of sense here. If you, or your partner, are sexually avoidant, I would recommend you begin by talking about the fears of sex and sexuality and about the behaviors that accompany the avoidance. Hopefully you will be able to create the safety to move toward more sexual contact and work through the feelings that come up.

It is important not to push too hard, and it is important not to live a static, non-sexual life. Incorporating the details I addressed with high and low desire patterns and resolving induction patterns will help tremendously. If a high desire person pushes for sex without first comforting themselves from within, they will be more apt to be met with resistance. If the sexually avoidant person begins to express more sexual desire, it will make it easier for the high desire person to stop pushing for sex.

Again, there are two major sides to the issue: the tendency to avoid intimacy and the tendency to use it as a fix or to prove something. If we are strong and secure within ourselves, we will be more able to both desire and risk intimacy. Intimacy will also be more real if we are extending ourselves from our inner strength and not coming from unconscious or addictive dependency patterns.

CHAPTER 22
UNDERSTANDING YOUR AROUSAL PATTERN

I coined the term "arousal pattern" to provide another way in which to view our attractions and preferences. While the term implies physical arousal, I use it to speak to the whole host of issues that describe the physical, emotional, mental, and spiritual basis for our attractions to others. My intent is to express that we have energetic preferences that are just as specific as our physical preferences. There is also a connection between these energetic preferences and our physical preferences. While our overall attraction to someone is generally based on energies and connections that are not physical, these increase their physical/sexual attractiveness to us.

We also have attractions that are expressed more by physical preferences. Understanding these, and how they impact the emotional or spiritual connections, gives us another way to view desire and attractions. Our energetic connections affect our physical arousal, and our physical arousal affects our energetic connections. Our attractions and our sexual arousal are not just objective truths—like being interested in this or that body type. Although this may be partly the case, our preferences are actually similar to our relationship patterns. Just as we might attract people and circumstances that mirror what is unresolved in our past, or our tendency to be attracted to our disowned selves, we are aroused based on a similar set of variables.

The term arousal pattern suggests that our psychological and spiritual issues drive our physical and sexual desire patterns, and there are larger psychological issues that comprise our physical preferences. Having deeper insights as to why we might have certain preferences adds another perspective on attractions and helps us work through them. Understanding the basis of our preferences also gives us personal insights that will help us grow emotionally and spiritually.

Arousal patterns can operate in ways that are similar to how primary and disowned selves operate—we tend to be attracted to things our own self or system is lacking. Just as we tend to be attracted to personalities that are opposite ours, we tend to be drawn to bodies that are different from ours. Beginning with a simplistic and purely physical description of an arousal pattern, we tend to be attracted to someone who is bigger or smaller than we are. It isn't always this simple, but this can be a good way to begin to understand this. The physical desire for someone who is bigger or smaller is an expression of an emotional state that is more comfortable for us. If someone is bigger than we are, it might unconsciously bring out feelings of vulnerability, as if the bigger person is a powerful figure who is caring for us. We might prefer bigger people if we desire being in a more receptive or submissive position in a relationship. If someone is smaller, it might bring out our feelings of power or dominance, or the desire to nurture. This might be more arousing to someone who likes to be in a giving mode, where being bigger helps them feel strong and powerful.

This is one way to explain why we all have different preferences. For example, while most heterosexual men might prefer women who are smaller than they are, it is definitely not the case that they all do. There are men and women who prefer people to be larger than them. It is important to note that I agree with the common notion that physical preferences, for example in favor of smaller women, are learned culturally. This is easily explained by how in some cultures having a larger body represents wealth or power, and is therefore more sexually desirable. But, I also feel that the physical cultural preferences exist because of emotional cultural preferences. I am hypothesizing that, for example, a man who was taught he should be more powerful and dominant than a woman is more likely to be attracted to a woman smaller than he is, whereas a man who was taught that it was more desirable to be receptive is more likely to be attracted to larger, more powerful women.

A woman might favor tall or large men because it supports her in feeling secure or receptive. Or, she might favor smaller men because she feels safer and more able to feel powerful. The preferences are also rooted in psychological issues, which the culture teaches us to prefer. By seeing these cultural and psychological connections, we can then work to have more control over what and who attracts us.

Physical Arousal Patterns

While I think a large portion of what attracts us is biological, I also think we can get some value by applying these same principles to our preferences for men or women, as well as penis, vaginal, or breast size. Heterosexuals have a sex drive that is a very simple expression of how we are attracted to what we don't have, or to energies that are complimentary. If we just look at the common differences between men and women's bodies, we can begin to see how it is partly the differences between the two bodies that make for heterosexual arousal. We might have a bigger or stronger body and be drawn to a smaller or softer one. We might have a body without much hair on it and be drawn to one with more hair. We might have a penis and the psychological and spiritual desire to impregnate, and therefore be drawn to the receptivity and fertility of a vagina. If we have a soft and receptive vagina, we might be drawn to the hard power of the penis.

With regard to heterosexual and bi-sexual men's interest in women's breasts, I have found some men who feel their interest in breasts to be connected to their desire to receive their mother's nurturing. Men who are more focused on giving, penetrating, or impregnating are more apt to focus on a woman's hips, vagina, and bottom, and may also tend to be less focused on breast size. Obviously, this theory is not as applicable to homosexuals, but I could use it to note that gays and lesbians do not have as many ways for their partner to physically represent their opposite or disowned self. Regardless, homosexuals do still have the potential for many of the opposites that this chapter mentions, such as size, age, wealth, and sexual preferences.

Any physical preference can be looked at as an arousal pattern. For example, if we prefer blonds we could ask ourselves what blonds represent to us. If we prefer darker hair, we can ask what it represents. I think it is possible that our culture's near obsession with blond women could be because we are taught blonds represent innocence and purity in much the same way redheads are believed to be fiery. Seeing this could help us let go of this and be more equally aroused by all hair colors.

Age preferences are also often part of an arousal pattern. Some people prefer older people, some younger, some the same age, and others don't care. While age may not matter, and it is the spirit or age of someone's heart that is most relevant to our attraction to them, it is also common to hypothesize that if someone is with an older person, it is because of parental issues. We might say, "He is old enough to be her father." The desire to subconsciously re-create our connection with a parent can be one source for an arousal pattern, where we prefer older people, but it can be even more helpful if we consider how age differences subconsciously elevate and lower someone's status or power in our eyes. Age may represent power. In general, age differences could be a way to experience power and giving and receiving issues. If we are with someone who is older than we are, we may be more comfortable being in a subservient or receptive position; and if we prefer being with people who are younger, we may prefer to be in a dominant or giving position.

Security Arousal Patterns

I have had a lifelong pattern of being attracted to older women. At times, I have problematized this arousal pattern by questioning whether this was an expression of unresolved issues about earning my mother's love and attention. I have wondered if I was more comfortable with older people because of how fast I had to grow up and be mature. I also think that by being with someone older, who I viewed as more responsible, I felt freer from the feeling I had to be in the nurturing role (which used to be my main pattern). While it can be valuable to think about our arousal patterns in this way, it is also okay just to enjoy what works for us.

In my early years, some of the women with whom I was in a relationship were significantly older, and at age twenty-three, I married Paula, who was eight years older. When I became single at age forty, I found that I continued to be attracted to older women, but I also found myself more interested in women of all ages. I had a five-year partnership with a woman who was eleven years younger.

Being in a relationship with people of different ages has given me the feeling that if my arousal pattern with older women was based on unresolved issues, then I have worked through them. I now find I am attracted to both older and younger women.

Money is another area where it is somewhat easy to quantify arousal patterns. There is a tendency to criticize people who are attracted to those who have more money. We call them "gold diggers." These judgments are often misguided, and it is better to view the attraction to people who have more or less money, income, or financial freedom in ways that are similar to what I expressed above regarding age. Sometimes people are subconsciously drawn to people with less money because it helps them feel powerful or nurturing. We are likely to be attracted to people with more money if we have the desire or need for security or to be taken care of.

In the end, I am distilling relationships down to issues of giving and receiving and suggesting that it is healthy to do both. It is unnecessary for us to judge someone harshly just because they are attracted to the power of someone's money. If someone is in relationship with someone who has more money, it may be because they are motivated by security issues and the power of the money makes them feel more secure. It would be helpful to make the distinction that security arouses them, not money. It is really no different from being attracted to someone because they are talkative, funny, well educated, big, or have a trait that is like any other disowned self of ours.

Sexual Arousal Patterns

Another important and perhaps deeper way I use the term arousal pattern is to describe why we prefer certain sex acts more than others. We all have emotional preferences that may be best experienced or satisfied by certain kinds of sexual experiences. This gives a deeper understanding of what drives our arousal because it helps us see that it is more than just the physical traits and experiences that enable us to feel the emotional state of love and arousal. Physicality can help us experience emotional states like the power or receiving issues I mentioned above, but it is not necessary. For example, having a smaller or more vulnerable body is not required in order to feel vulnerable, or allow yourself to be held and to receive. A large man can be held by a small woman and feel receptive or submissive. A man and a woman of the same size can take turns feeling big or little. Obviously, the same is true in same sex relationships.

Focusing on preferred sexual experiences more than on physical differences also makes it easier to include homosexual relationships into this discussion. While the physical examples in the preceding pages may have seemed to exclude homosexuals, I think that many homosexual men and women are better able to relate to what I am expressing when I discuss size, power, and giving and receiving issues. There are many ways to accomplish these feelings, even if both bodies might have similar size or muscle content. I do not have a bias that we are supposed to be attracted to our opposite, as there are many advantages, whether you are heterosexual or homosexual, to being attracted to someone who is similar to you.

Most sexual desires and experiences can be distilled down to acts that satisfy our desire to give or feel powerful, and acts that satisfy our desire to be vulnerable or receive. Some people will also get value by adding the term dominance to the giving side of this and the word submission to the receiving side of this. Giving (power and dominance) and receiving (vulnerability and submission) are central to relationships of all kinds, including sexual relationships. In sexual intercourse, for example, most people report that they can more easily feel powerful or in a giving mode if they are on top, and that if they are on the bottom they may more likely feel vulnerable or receptive. This explains why so many people prefer being on top; it is easier for many people to orgasm if they are in the more powerful position. Also, if someone has the tendency to be triggered by abuse memories, they might feel safer on top because the bottom might activate the vulnerability that was part of the original abuse.

There are similar and more pronounced issues with oral sex. Many people are more comfortable giving oral sex than receiving it. Receiving it is more vulnerable because we are letting someone closer to our core, both physically and emotionally. There are additional issues that make oral sex more complicated for women. Women may have been subliminally taught that their vaginas are dirty and smelly, and they may fear letting it be kissed. On the other hand, women need the more direct stimulation that oral sex provides, so this may motivate them to resolve the receiving issues.

The history of sexual abuse and sexual objectification issues may contribute to women not enjoying giving oral sex. It is hard to want something by which you have historically felt pressured, probed, chased, or objectified. Women can understandably be uncomfortable taking the force and power of a penis into their mouths.

Further, I have come to feel that men have ruined women's experience of giving oral sex by pushing their masculine need to give, thrust, and dominate into it. I would prefer to see oral sex's innate nature as being about receiving and being vulnerable, and about giving love and devotion. I have been shocked to hear many women describe men as being aggressive and thrusting their penis into the woman's mouth, and that men tend to be unable to surrender and receive oral sex. As one woman put it, "Men treat women's mouths as just another orifice to _____."

Women's stories range from men wanting to be upright in a dominant position, with the woman on her knees, to men grabbing women's heads as they orgasm in an attempt to force the woman to swallow! This is a serious violation of trust. Just because sex begins consensually does not mean every act has been given consent. The process of making love is done together, and trying new things needs to be done with sensitivity and communication. It should be obvious that if someone is gasping for air or wincing in pain there is a problem.

Men and women need to get out of this pattern and learn to trust each other and open to the vulnerability of receiving oral sex. This will most often result in the receiver being on their back and not making many strong movements. Given that a less extreme part of the masculine pattern is to prefer giving or penetrating, it will feel alien for many men to learn to lie back and receive. Receiving oral sex is the opposite of the male tendency to want to penetrate, and we need to learn to let our partner in as we receive oral sex.

I had a client who often had to imagine that he was giving to his partner or having intercourse with her, just to be able to maintain an erection or to orgasm. He felt great accomplishment when he was able to relax and be aroused by the act of receiving oral sex. For him to think about receiving oral sex instead of fantasizing about giving to, or penetrating his partner, gave him a vehicle to learn how to receive and let love in. It was a symbol that he was growing psychologically, and it was not just his primary pattern of giving that aroused him.

For women it is similar. Receiving oral sex is the opposite of being a dutiful caregiver. It is the opposite of being dirty and bad for wanting sex. To receive is to know and value our juices. The act of learning to receive oral sex can be a great metaphor for believing that we and our sexuality are good, and we are worthy of receiving. It takes trust to open our legs and let someone that close to our core. Oral sex is a way to express trust and connection with our partner.

137

I have always found it interesting that one of the most erotic things some of us can think of is to place our mouth where our mother and our culture taught us was dirty. Reversing the taboo or notion that our partners' genitals are dirty is an aspect of why it turns us on to kiss them. What a unique way to express unconditional love. It is as if we are saying to them, "I love all of you, and all of you is clean and innocent." A similar but more spiritual description is that it is beautiful for our partner to let us into their core that way. When they let us kiss or suck them, they are letting us see and touch their most vulnerable spots. By touching them with our mouth and tongue, we are giving them honor and respect.

Oral sex can feel like a form of personal worship, and as such, it can be very arousing. The same is true with sexual intercourse. To penetrate, or be penetrated, and be touching our partner's core with ours while looking into their eyes is sacred. It satisfies our most basic desire to merge and be intimate with another.

Sexual intercourse where we penetrate or are penetrated from behind, offers some specific metaphors. Many men and women like this very much, as it empowers the person penetrating to feel even more powerful than they do being on top, with their bodies chest to chest. For the person being penetrated, it offers the ability to let their partner in and "take" them or dominate them in a deep way. For heterosexuals, it offers some added power spiritually, because in this position the woman's sacred spot or "G spot" on the inside of her vagina and the more sensitive front of the man's penis are receiving more contact.

Some people are not comfortable being penetrated from behind. Many have reported that it feels too submissive and vulnerable. For some, it may bring up abuse or sexual objectification issues. It is important to honor these feelings, and it is up to the individuals to decide if they want to try to work through them and learn to experience it as a positive way to receive.

Our arousal pattern in the area of sex acts is not just about the acts themselves; it is the energy being expressed that attracts us. It is not what you do, it is how you do it that is most important. If someone is penetrating their partner with anger, it will not feel safe. If someone who feels vulnerable being penetrated from behind is being penetrated with strong, instinctual power, it will be more challenging than if their partner begins with softer energy.

We might imagine a couple beginning gently in this position, and then over time the one on top might express more power. Eventually one might be pushing down on the other's back, or pulling on their hips while the one on the bottom is pushing and thrusting backwards. Both partners might access unexplored feelings and emotions if they allow themselves to explore new territory and use enthusiastic words and sounds that describe the power or receptivity of their experience. If we describe a position, it says little. The energy we express is equally or more important. If someone said, "I was on top, and we had beautiful eye contact," it only partly explains their lovemaking. They could be on top, moving gently and not talking, or they could be on top, moving aggressively, and saying passionate things. Saying we made love, even if we add the position, says little. The actual experience varies with the energy we express. There are many details to our preferences and what they represent to us. As we move into new territory, we enter new areas of personal growth.

Who Initiates?

Another important area of arousal patterns is the tendency to prefer being the initiator of sex versus having our partner initiate it. If one person does all the initiating, the desire patterns are more likely to get stuck. Relationships will grow and remain open on more levels if sex is initiated and desired somewhat equally. Men and women both have their own stereotypical issues to address here. Men need to slow down and give women more room. They need to get comfortable with more nonsexual intimacy and foreplay and to stop pushing sex. Women need to get comfortable with their power, gain confidence, and deal with their fear of rejection. As initiators of relationships, men have had to deal with performance anxiety and the fear of being rejected. Men have always taken more risks than we realize, and we need to acknowledge them for that. Because our cultures tend to put women in the passive role, where they did not initiate relationships as often, women have not had to confront their performance anxieties and rejection issues as directly. The old stereotype that a woman who wants sex is a "slut" needs to be resolved by everyone. It takes a great deal of courage for women to let go of the old norms and become initiators, and they need to be acknowledged for that. When both partners initiate sex, they are both more likely to feel loved and wanted. This creates increased security and self-esteem.

There are also reasons that are not as gender-based, which make us prefer to initiate sex or prefer our partner to initiate it. These are about giving vs. receiving, or power vs. vulnerability. When we initiate sex, we are more likely to be in the role of giving, but we are also more able to express our power or dominance. When we are receiving our partner's advances, we are more able to connect with our feelings of vulnerability or submission.

Many couples have conflict in this area, where one of them feels like they are always being pursued and that there is not room for them to be the pursuer. This issue is similar to the idea of preferring being on top, and it is important to take turns to allow our partner room to initiate so that they can be in their power. If they are always responding to our advances, and their primary arousal pattern is to be powerful also, they might end up having less desire. If we back off enough and let them initiate, then they could begin to explore their desire more closely, and the result would be that it would develop. Taking turns is important, especially if our arousal patterns are similar.

Other Factors

Abandonment issues are also a big topic with arousal patterns. Our fear of abandonment can make us select a partner whom we would be less afraid might leave us or have an affair. We might feel more secure if our partner were more submissive, introverted, conservatively dressed, had less sex drive, was not financially prosperous or free, or anything else that might feel threatening. The more we work on our self-esteem and our ability to self-soothe, the more comfortable we become in being attracted to people we perceive to be powerful.

Likewise the opposite is true; if someone is extremely attractive and has the appearance of a "trophy," they are more apt to attract people who seek to conquer and possess love. There is a feeling in the psychological community that women who possess and express a trophy level of beauty are more apt to attract abusive men who seek to control them. The same idea should be considered with financial power or fame and applied to beautiful or powerful men and women as well. This theory may also be explained by how it is natural for people's arousal patterns to be suppressed or intimidated by powerful or beautiful people, so the more average "nice guys" are more likely to be afraid to approach beautiful women. The end result is that the people who are willing to take on the challenge of approaching someone of power or trophy level beauty are apt to include a higher percentage of "controllers and abusers."

This does not mean that extremely beautiful people are doomed; however, it *does* mean that beautiful people could benefit from understanding that their beauty may intimidate many people. I suggest that the more beautiful or powerful someone is, the more they should take on the role of initiating relationships because by doing so, they will more likely reach people who would be interested in them but who are afraid of making contact or afraid of rejection.

An *unavailability pattern* is another term I frequently use, which fits into this discussion. This is a good way to describe how we may be motivated to chase those who are unavailable, and people who are unavailable can hook us into chasing them. There are many reasons we attract or are attracted to unavailable people. (I will be addressing these reasons in greater detail in Chapter 25.) These reasons include our seeking to prove our worth or to break down barriers we felt with our parents. Regardless of the reasons, we may be attracted to married people, workaholics, addicts, long distance relationships, or to people who are emotionally unavailable. The term unavailability pattern is a good way to summarize and admit the issue and help us remember to turn our focus to those who are available.

Arousal Patterns and Affairs

If we are in a partnership, how does our arousal pattern affect our attractions and our ability to be monogamous? Arousal patterns motivate us to have affairs in the same ways disowned selves do. We tend to be attracted to the opposite of who we are or what we have. We will be attracted to people with qualities that differ from our partner even if they were not our original preference. It helps to realize that if we were to leave our partner or have an affair to seek these qualities, once we had them we would likely return to our original preference. Most importantly, we can, and should, work on developing the qualities we are lacking in our existing relationship. This applies to all physical traits, personality qualities, and relationship experiences.

Here are a few examples:

David had always preferred women with small breasts, and his partner Stacy had small breasts. After being with Stacy for a few years, David found himself increasingly attracted to women with bigger breasts. This is a natural expression of his system seeking things that it does not have. It is not a big deal, and by viewing it in this way he realized that once he had a relationship with someone with larger breasts, he would likely return to his original preference for smaller breasts. While David understood this was a superficial issue, realizing this helped him let go of his attraction to women with bigger breasts and let go of his fantasy of having an affair with one. It also helped David let go of his interest in having Stacy get implants.

Carolyn originally preferred gentle or subdued men because more expressive or extroverted men subconsciously reminded her of her chaotic or verbally abusive past. She married Brian, who was a gentle and quiet man. As their marriage grew, she began to judge Brian for being too introverted. She wanted more contact and expression in their relationship. Brian also wanted to be more expressive and have more communication in their relationship. He felt his gentle or subdued personality was something he had developed to protect himself from rejection. Together, Carolyn and Brian began to get more comfortable with intimacy in general. Carolyn worked to feel safe with Brian's expression and power on all levels, and Brian worked to feel safe to express himself and be seen in the world.

Naomi and Alex both preferred gentle sex because it felt more sacred and in alignment with their spiritual ideals. They reached a phase in their life where they noticed they were attracted to others who they perceived to be more free and powerful sexually, and they each wanted more power or instinct in their sex life. They did not need to seek new lovers. They worked with this together within their partnership and experimented with how it felt to have stronger, more expressive sex. They enjoyed using their sex life to tap new instincts and become more powerful on many levels. While they enjoyed the benefit of new kinds of sexual expression, their original preference for gentle sex did remain dominant. By incorporating both gentle and powerful sex, they were less distracted or aroused by people who they perceived to be more sexually dynamic.

This chapter also brings up the complex point that as we grow, our arousal pattern will grow, leaving us attracted to people and qualities that our partner does not have as dominant. Most often recognizing this as a disowned self and not acting on it is the best choice. Other times it might be time to move on because our original arousal pattern was based on issues that no longer serve us.

For example: Stephanie had a history of being attracted to men who she viewed as more powerful than herself. Most of the men she dated were much older, and a few of them were well known in the community as well as financially prosperous. They also tended to be verbally dominant while she was quieter and more submissive. She married James, who was seventeen years her senior and controlled many aspects of their lives. She found herself falling out of love with him and growing increasingly angry with him for being dominant. She understood that she used to be more comfortable in the submissive position because she wanted to be taken care of but that she was also growing out of it as she grew into her own power.

Stephanie tried to confront various imbalances in their relationship, but James was unwilling to work on making room for her to have and express more power in the ways they lived and communicated. Eventually she decided to leave. Leaving in this case could be seen as a healthy step in her growth. She went forward in life to create more of an equal, and she was ready to do so because she was committed to letting go of her own subservient side and embrace her power.

The same kind of example can also illustrate this point from the opposite perspective. If a man or woman were attracted to people who were subservient because of a desire to remain safe and in control, the more they resolved their control issues, the more they would develop a healthy attraction to people who they felt were more powerful. If they were in a relationship with someone who wasn't willing to work with assuming more power and responsibility in the relationship, they might eventually need to leave the relationship in order to grow.

It is common for people to leave relationships before working on these issues. If we do leave, we tend to carry the issues with us, so it is best to work on incorporating opposites into existing relationships. Ultimately, it is a personal choice as to whether we choose to make changes within an existing relationship or if we feel it might be more practical to leave a relationship to more easily accomplish what we need.

My awareness of arousal patterns (and of disowned selves) has helped me understand that differences are part of attraction and are therefore part of successful relationships. But this awareness has also led me to

146

conclude that relationships work best when they are somewhat equal. We will always fantasize about and be attracted to opposites and things we don't have, but I find that when relationships have equality and common ground, they function best and last the longest. It is good news that equal does not mean the same. Within the themes in this section of sexual desire, giving and receiving, a couple will achieve the most personal growth if they take turns somewhat equally. This can be applied to many other areas of a relationship: sexuality, money, and communication, as well as to topics less central to arousal patterns, such as chores, child rearing, and bill paying. If we become aware of our differences and incorporate our partner's ways, we will create a more equal flow of energy between us. When the energy flows back and forth, relationships last.

CHAPTER 23
FANTASY BONDING

Fantasy bonding is the tendency to bond or attach to the fantasy of whom we project or hope a person to be instead of loving who they really are. Our image of them may not be entirely real. It may be based on who we need them to be. Fantasy bonding is actually natural and inevitable to a degree because it is natural for our vulnerable side to need people to be good, nurturing, and available to us, or anything else we might need.

When we "fall in love," we are partly bonding with our fantasy or projection of who we want someone to be. Instead of "falling in love," I encourage people to "rise in love." Falling in love implies that we want someone to catch us. When we are strong and secure in the world, we are less likely to project our fantasies on to others. Addressing our "fantasy bonds" also helps us learn to start relationships with both feet on the ground instead of rushing into a relationship out of the need to be in one, or out of unconscious dependency. If relationships are going to last and be monogamous, we need to come to terms with how fantasies can lead us to run away in search of something new. Working with this issue is also critical for real intimacy. Real intimacy happens in reality with both feet on the ground, not in fantasy.

As I said earlier, the original fantasy bond is with our parents because as children we needed to feel that there was someone doing a good job taking care of us so we could feel safe and secure in the world. As a result, if there was something lacking within our parents' performance, we would deny those feelings and instead fantasize that they were better parents than they actually were. We may have done this with one parent more than the other. We might have admitted that one parent had shortcomings that upset us but fantasized about the other, thinking that they were a better parent than they really were. It is too scary to admit that both parents were unavailable or abusive, so sometimes we make one parent the good one and one the bad one.

As we grow, fantasy bonds continue. When we have a crush on someone, we are fantasizing that they would be perfect for us. As adults, we might plan a date with someone and even before the date have grand notions about how wonderful they are. Then after many dates, if we think we are falling in love, part of the process is that we are falling in love with our image of them. Much of this image is based on who we want or need them to be, and not on who they really are. We are bonding to them, but we are also bonding to our fantasy of who we hope they are.

We also do this in non-sexual relationships. We need good friends, so we might stretch our image of someone beyond reality and into fantasy. We do this with things when we imagine the car or vacation home that will help us feel better. We do it with cities when we think that if we move it will be better. We do it with jobs or organizations.

Again, it is because our vulnerable side needs a good partner, job, and place to live.

Our positive feelings are valid, but being aware of the tendency to fantasize means that it might be a good idea to slow down in relationships and allow ourselves to discover who the person is. If we slow down and adjust our image of a person slightly downward, we will have both feet on the ground. This will result in deeper and more authentic contact because we will be rising in love with more of who the person really is and less of who we want them to be.

I still respect and encourage deep love. People feel and express love differently. If we are a warm, generous, and passionate person, we should continue to be ourselves. Note how many problems I have addressed in this book that are about the opposite tendency. I do not recommend that we fear, suppress, and avoid our desire because of the fear of loss. If we do, we are unable to be intimate. If we love deeply and quickly, there is much that is good about that, but we will probably be best served if we can create a balance. If we are passionate and tend to attract people who are in some way our opposite, we may end up with someone who is more cautious and expresses love less vigorously than we do. If this happens, we will be well served to slow down and work on our fantasy bond.

A key to slowing down and not projecting our fantasies on to others is for us to meet our own needs and continually address our dependency issues. Just because someone loves deeply and quickly does not mean they are dependant. We all have a dependent side, and remembering to self-soothe is a key to being ourselves and creating a balance. Whatever stage a relationship is in, we need to meet our own needs and let go of the part of us that hopes the other person will save us.

Not everyone fantasy bonds to the same degree. We all also have varying degrees of the opposite pattern, which would be to judge others. Judging people, or focusing on their imperfections, can be a way of staying isolated, safe, and independent. Some people have this pattern more than the tendency to fantasy bond. If this is the case, self-soothing will result in action steps that would involve learning to express love and take more risks; whereas if we want to resolve our tendency to fantasy bond, the steps involve slowing down.

Another way to describe why fantasy bonding causes problems is that if we rush into a relationship and quickly have grand notions of how wonderful the other person is, our love will not feel real to them. They will feel like we couldn't possibly know them that well that fast, and they will feel a lack of reality. They will then be likely to feel or project that we are just looking for a relationship and that we do not genuinely want them. This can lead to them feeling objectified, and they may feel our love is controlling or possessive. They will feel our desire to love deeply but will be unable to believe it is real because they will not feel that you are really able to know them and love them that deeply in such a short time.

There is no need to outlaw fantasy or worry explicitly about the degree to which we are in fantasy vs. reality. There is innocence in allowing some fantasy. It is also inevitable that the fantasy bond will always be one component of relationships, but it is not the only reason we love deeply. By remembering that it is just one component, we will also be able to relax and let love develop. Love also needs enthusiasm and spontaneity to grow. If we were to eliminate the spontaneous and joyous celebration of loving and finding or dating someone about whom we are excited, we would cause a different but equal problem. If we are beginning a relationship, and we do not allow ourselves to be excited, or if we require that all steps have to be slow, real, and grounded, then we might stifle the process of forming the connection.

If someone approached us for a second or third date in a completely dry, business like way, it would be discouraging to the part of us that wants to be wanted. We might want the person to be real and have both feet on the ground, but we also want them to be excited about us. We need both a sense of reality and excitement.

Perhaps the biggest value of letting go of fantasy bonds is that it helps us face the reality of our life and of our childhood. By letting go of the tendency to idealize our parents and others, we have another way to begin to look at our core feelings and resolve them. The more able we are to nurture ourselves and the more secure we are in the world, the more able we are to do this work. Most people idealize and fantasize more frequently earlier in life than later. The strength to let go of fantasy goes hand and hand with deeper engagement in personal growth. This kind of depth is necessary to sustain vital monogamous relationships.

CHAPTER 24
THE DISOWNED SELF OF YOUR RELATIONSHIP

I have already discussed how primary and disowned selves affect attractions when I described how Sharon and Patricia represented disowned selves that forced me to admit that I felt there were things lacking in my marriage. The tendency to have attractions to a disowned self explains a major difficulty with maintaining monogamous relationships.

If you have a partner, realize that they were once a disowned self, and you probably felt much joy as you joined with them because their opposites made you feel more complete. Now, perhaps years later, you and your partner are your own relationship system, with a primary self of its own, and you probably have a new opposite, to which you will likely be attracted. In my case, when I met Paula I was young, relatively free of responsibility, and was not very established financially. I craved responsibility, structure, and power when I was originally attracted to her, but years later, I became more attracted to spontaneous people or images. Spontaneity became the opposite of the long-term responsible marriage we had created. I used this theory to work through my attractions by developing the qualities that I was attracted to within myself, learning to create them within my current relationship, and by avoiding the temptation to see the people I was attracted to as a fix. I sought to create the qualities I desired in my current life and relationship.

We can be more proactive by calculating what the disowned self of our relationship is before we even meet someone who fits the description. We can take our current situation and almost mathematically figure out to what we will be drawn. We will be drawn to things that our current relationship lacks. If we're in a partnership, being prepared for this will help us be conscious of what is driving our attractions before we even develop a crush. By doing this, we can address the issues that are lacking or are underdeveloped in our relationship before we even have strong attractions. This will also help us respond to the people to whom we're attracted in a more mature way and leave us better able to maintain our monogamy, if that is our choice.

If we're single, this is a good question to ask, too. Based on our past and perhaps our last relationship, to what qualities or energies are we likely to be attracted? This won't only affect the kind of person we're looking at or fantasizing about; it will affect whom we attract, or with whom the universe pairs us. Earlier I mentioned how people with chaotic or abusive pasts tend to seek or attract relationships with stable or responsible people. Once those stable or responsible qualities become more primary, whether within ourselves or within a present or past relationship, we will tend to seek more feeling or spontaneity.

Another example would be if our past or present partner wanted sex all the time. In that case, we might tend to want someone who is less sexual. If things have been too focused on money, we will subconsciously crave someone to whom finances are a lesser priority. If our partner had a particular communication style, we would tend to attract someone who was his or her opposite.

The qualities we seek are also like a system or a group of qualities. For example, if our past or present partner was or is an emotionally suppressed, financially driven extrovert, you will tend to be attracted to someone who is more introverted yet also freer emotionally and who is not as driven by money.

CHAPTER 25
THE INCEST TABOO

The incest taboo is a multifaceted and far-reaching pattern, which plays havoc on relationships. In many families, the fear of incest or of being inappropriately sexual results in physical and emotional distance. This issue causes families to numb their intimate connections with their children in an effort to ensure that they do not become sexually inappropriate. This results in life long patterns of avoiding intimacy and sexuality, especially with the people with whom we live. The incest taboo creates a duality where we can't be close to the people with whom we live because they represent our family, and it is important not to be sexual with our family. On the other hand, we can be sexual with those outside our family, so it is a subconscious reason people have affairs.

Discussing sexual taboos from childhood in this way is not appropriate for individuals with a history of sexual abuse. This pattern should not be applied to those recovering from incest. While everyone can benefit from counseling, a history of childhood sexual abuse is an area where counseling is an essential aspect of healing. It is also important for childhood abuse survivors not to pressure themselves to address the issues without the support of a therapist.

It is even taboo to talk about the incest taboo. A premise of addressing the taboo is that it is normal to notice that our children are cute, and it is possible that any intimate relationship (even with our children) will lead to our being aware of sexual feelings. Most people are uncomfortable with this notion. A first step in healing the taboo is to realize that there is a complete and total difference between loving our children and having the awareness of them as sexual beings, and how a pedophile would react to intimacy with a child. My assertion is that if we are open to having a loving experience with almost anyone, but especially someone whom we love deeply, some awareness of sexuality is likely. The key issue is that if we are working to make sure incest doesn't happen, we will tend to withdraw from the intimate and emotional connection with our children.

I use the term incest taboo in the context of describing how noticing our children as sexually attractive beings scares us. Imagine a father, much like yours, who probably came from a religious ethic of working to be, and be seen as, a good person. Then, one day, when his daughter is sitting on his lap, he notices her as a sexual being. This takes him by complete surprise; he freaks out, decides it's wrong, removes his daughter, and never allows her to return to his lap. As time goes on, he makes sure to distance himself from any situation that might bring sexual feelings to the surface. By the time his daughter is a young woman, they have intense arguments that are rationalized as her being a rebellious teenager. What is actually occurring during the teenage years is that he is picking fights with her because it is just too uncomfortable for him to notice how beautiful she is.

Beginning with her loss of her daddy's lap, she feels confused and rejected. She will likely have unconscious feelings that there must be something wrong with her. Depending upon the additional phobias the particular family places on the body or on sexuality, she will conclude that her sexuality or her body must be bad.

The same is true for boys. With boys, the first key moment might be the point where their mother felt uncomfortable helping them bathe. Whether we are boys or girls, as our mother or father bathed us, we might have noticed a change in their energy as they touch our genitals. Even if they didn't panic and stop bathing us, this explains one way the incest taboo is transmitted and teaches us sexual taboos. If our parents withdrew their energy as they bathed our genitals or breasts, it communicated that our genitals or breasts had some mysterious importance and were somehow negative. As our parents withdrew their energy from our genitals, we got the message that our genitals were bad. Note that this feeling gets stronger as it is combined with a host of other negative family and social messages that implied that genitals were bad or dirty.

Children have a natural tendency to be curious and a desire to explore, and being curious about their parents' bodies and sexuality can be a normal part of this. Some children want to touch their mother's breasts or their father's penis. They may also want to see their parents naked. If a parent gets overly uncomfortable with this, it just adds to the taboos about our bodies and our sexuality. Curiosity is normal, and many parents make the error of shaming their children for it in an effort to create firm boundaries. This does not mean that parents should allow children to touch them; it means that parents should not shame their children. Most often, it is appropriate for the parent to simply say, "Sorry honey, I am not comfortable with you touching me there; that's my body, breast, penis, etc." Notice that having this boundary can become part of how we can teach our kids that they can say no to unwanted touch.

It is also normal for parents to notice that their children are beautiful human beings. It is normal for parents to have some awareness of their own sexuality when intimate with their children. This does not mean that the parents are at risk of molesting a child. Instead of relaxing about the issue and maintaining an intimate connection, parents often get uncomfortable and break contact with their children physically, emotionally, or both—resulting in a sense of rejection and a feeling that our sexuality is bad and inappropriate, which affects our adult relationships. Also note that if parents relax about their sexual feelings, the feelings subside—the more they disown them, the more volcanic they become.

Let me add that a child isn't concerned with sexuality; they just want connection. Throughout all of this, they have no reason to feel that there is any problem. They just want to be intimate and connected with the parent, and they see no reason for not being close. As a result, they take any distancing very personally.

This taboo on our sexuality creates a whole host of adult patterns. The most basic pattern is having less sex. Feeling that sex is bad results in avoiding it. This can take an extreme of celibacy or even living one's entire life as a virgin. I have worked with countless people who felt the incest taboo explained their sexual history. For example, it explains the tendency for sex to diminish with marriage or when two people move in together. The principle here is that when our relationship evolves and closely resembles a family, the subconscious notions that sex is wrong enters into the picture.

When we were children, it was wrong to be sexual with our parents or siblings, so when someone subconsciously resembles a parent or sibling, the taboo surfaces, and we start to make love less often. Someone can subconsciously resemble a family member as soon as we're monogamous, when we move in with her or him, when we get married, or it can take many years to surface. Often it comes up out of nowhere after we have been married the same number of years as the age we were when an earlier abandonment occurred, such as the original lap or bathing incident. If a parent shut us out when we were seven, it might be the seventh year of marriage that brings up the issue. The subconscious can be extremely specific in the way it replays patterns.

The incest taboo also explains one major reason people create relationship triangles or have affairs. Notice that when we were children, it was known that it wouldn't be permissible for us to marry or have sex with a parent or sibling. But whom could we marry? Someone else, like the boy or girl next door. As adults, our primary partner becomes taboo sexually because we subconsciously feel that they are a family member, and we subconsciously feel bad about making love with them. Affairs are "okay" because they represent the innocence of the boy or girl next door. This explains part of why we might feel excited about the newness of the affair—there is actually a feeling that it is more innocent and less taboo.

The other side of this is how we can attract a partner that has an affair. As children, we may be used to being the outsider and feeling excluded from the intimacy our parents shared. So, having the exclusive attention of our adult partner is unfamiliar, and we are more receptive to our partner having an affair or leaving us for another. This is because their leaving us or having an affair reproduces the separation or abandonment and the old familiar feelings that there must be something wrong with us, sexually or otherwise.

This also begins to explain the third corner of a relationship triangle, which is being the third person as a means of competing to win our parents' love. Up to this point, I have been illustrating ways of acting out or repeating the rejection issues, but the opposite is also true: Feelings of rejection can motivate us to compensate and compete for love to prove our worth. This is the sexual equivalent of, "He who dies with the most toys wins." Here it takes the form of sexual conquest, like he who has the most lovers has proven himself worthy of his mother's (or father's) love.

When we have a relationship with someone who is unavailable, it is likely we are expressing some unresolved parental issues. The most basic are proving our desirability, innocence, or worthiness. The incest taboo results in our feeling isolated or rejected by our parents. We can then be compelled to break through that isolation by breaking down the barrier that unavailability represents to us. It is as if we want the unavailable person to leave their partner (or job or city) for us, and if they do, it would prove our worth and erase the original feelings of rejection we felt with our parents.

This can also take the form of sexual conquest in general, where having many sex partners is an unconscious attempt to prove your worth or prove that sex is innocent and okay. Sometimes motives for sex become like earning points or notches on your belt. If we view conquest as earning points, we could see creating intimate contact with a single person as worth one point. Married people might be worth ten points, etc. Looking back on our past, how many points have we scored? How many points do we need to score before we feel good enough as a man or woman? Sometimes it might take seventy single people, or maybe fifty single people and two married ones, or maybe just one priest or nun would settle the score!

The incest taboo also results in feeling that sex is dirty. This creates a taboo on sexual desire and might cause us to suppress our desire, as if it is bad or dirty. If a partner or potential partner responds too enthusiastically, we might feel that there is something wrong with them. For example, if a man asks a woman for sex and she says, "Sure, just let me stop by my house and get my sex toys," the man might feel that she didn't respond the way his mother would have; therefore, she must be a slut. These feelings also affect the range within which we feel comfortable expressing ourselves in bed or the range within which we need our partner to stay to maintain our comfort. If our partner is too enthusiastic, do we shut down as if it was wrong to be excited and sexual or vice versa?

CHAPTER 26
RESOLVING THE TABOO

The solution to the incest taboo is to lighten up about sex and realize that sex and sexuality are normal and innocent. Innocence is required if we are going to continue to maintain an existing sexual connection and let go of the volcanoes that can sabotage our relationships. Innocence is a broad and sometimes vague word that describes the state we would naturally feel in the absence of guilt and shame. It may be easy to intellectualize that our sexuality is a normal part of being human, but really experiencing this is different. The main resolution is to resolve the old negatives by feeling them and choosing out of the beliefs and unsupportive behaviors associated with them. We can also develop innocence by acting innocent. Ask yourself, "How do I experience my innocence?" Initially you may have difficulty answering this, but the answers are the activities in which you engage that help you feel the absence of guilt. In general, they are probably things like taking a nap, walk, or bath, playing, or looking at something beautiful. In the area of sexuality, they are things like learning to enjoy sex and really be present while making love.

Oversexed behaviors, such as having affairs or using too much pornography (which might be any porn), can be a way to try to prove sex is innocent, but they end up adding to the guilt. Really being emotionally present while making love can be a means of learning that our sexuality is normal, appropriate, healthy, and spiritual.

In addition to this and the ideas in the previous sections, I have some specific suggestions, some of which might be controversial. Please only try them if you are comfortable with them, and remember to respect your own ethics and morals.

I can explain the need for the above warning by beginning with my more unique suggestion, which is to notice that your parents and siblings are attractive. If you have any attraction to them, it is helpful if you allow the feeling or even the fantasy. Just as the feelings behind any fantasy are innocent, all feelings are innocent. It can be helpful to discuss this with your partner or therapist as a means of getting the taboo further into the open. The purpose of this is simply to create innocence around the idea that it would be okay to desire our parents or siblings, thus okay to desire the person with whom we live, with whom we may be having difficulties sexually because of the unconscious taboos.

If the idea of finding a parent attractive disgusts you, I would suggest that you get a picture of them that was from the period when you were a child and the incest taboo was at its peak. Back then, they may have been very desirable. You might even notice that they look similar to the people to whom you tend to be most attracted now. Also, remember that this idea should not be directly applied to people who are recovering from incest. Incest survivors could hear this as my suggesting that it was normal for an abuser to have acted on any feelings of attraction, and they might hear this idea as my condoning their abuser's behavior, which I am not. More specifically, the suggestion of imagining a parent (or other predator) as attractive could be damaging for them. Remember that my whole discussion of the incest taboo does not apply to pedophiles.

If the taboo has resulted in avoiding sex or sex becoming less frequent, my most basic suggestion is to schedule sex. This may feel depressing, like we're admitting that we've lost sexual spontaneity. Most people in long-term relationships have lost some spontaneity, and scheduling sex is the most practical way to insure that sex occurs, especially with busy schedules and children. Most people find that once aroused, they feel very spontaneous regardless of how the foreplay was initiated. This may not resolve more serious patterns that result in an aversion to foreplay, but in many cases, scheduling sex will help.

Remember that you might work the taboo out in your dreams by having dreams where you have sex with family members or others who would be inappropriate sex partners that represented the taboo. There is no need to be alarmed by this. In fact, having incestuous dreams would be a sign of your accepting your sexuality and an indication that you are lightening up about the incest taboo.

Given that the incest taboo results in unconscious fear that sexuality and sex are bad, it also results in feelings that our bodies are somehow bad, dirty, or ugly. It can therefore be valuable to get comfortable with nudity. Anything that helps us relax about our bodies is helpful. With this suggestion, too, we should incorporate this only if it works for our boundaries and us. Hot springs, nude beaches, and resorts generally encourage nudity in a non-exhibitionist way.

It is also valuable to get better at handling the incest taboo with children. If parents stop passing sexual phobias on to their kids, it will make for a better world and a more evolved species. Being honest and open about sexuality also helps the parent recover from sexual taboos. Handling the issue properly with our children involves being honest about our feelings and admitting if we get uncomfortable. For example, with lap or bath time, the key if we get uncomfortable is just to admit it and try not to shut down. Our children will sense our discomfort anyway, and if we admit it, we will be more able to relax. If we're still uncomfortable and need to remove our child from our lap, for example, our child would not take it personally in the same way they would if we were not admitting our feelings. All we have to do is say, "Honey, I'm just not comfortable having you on my lap right now." By owning our feelings, they will get the message that the issue is about us and not because they did something wrong.

Another value of parents understanding the incest taboo is that it will help them create a relaxed atmosphere about nudity and enable them to give their children a more positive attitude about their bodies. This will result in all family members having an increased sense of sexual innocence. It is valuable to find an appropriate but not rigid boundary with nudity, where some nudity is natural. This does not mean that nudity should be pushed on the children or that the parents should remain nude if anyone is uncomfortable. Nudity can be exhibitionism, which is a kind of sexual abuse.

Understanding some basic child development issues can help parents distinguish the difference between nudity and exhibitionism. Young children are felt in child development circles to be natural nudists. This is an aspect of their exploratory nature. As children, most of us have played "doctor." It is helpful if the parents of small children are relaxed about being seen nude and relaxed if the child likes to be nude. Usually around the age of seven, there is an increased need for privacy on the child's part, and parents need to take a cue from the child and wear more clothing.

The next big area of concern as our children grow is in having a relaxed dialogue about sexuality. Parents need to be open but not pushy. If we're lucky, our children will talk to us about relationships. While it is normal that adolescents don't share much personal information, it is also important to try to talk to them. Talking to adolescents is similar to talking to smaller children about their feelings; usually it will feel like we as a parent are doing most of the talking. This is true because children of all ages are less able to articulate what they feel, and it helps them if the parent verbally identifies the emotion they are exhibiting.

If a child is upset, we can help them by putting words to the upset for them. We might say, "Wow, you are really disappointed." This helps them feel heard and integrate what they are feeling. Adolescents also talk less because they have a genuine need for privacy, and their need for independence results in them disowning the part of them that needs us. It is as if adolescents pretend that they don't need us, and we need to honor that and at the same time stay present with them.

It is important that we come from a relaxed place and let go of our own parental investments, which can result in being too dominant or controlling in our children's lives. If kids sense our judgment, we have no chance of hearing anything about their adolescent challenges. Even if we're opened, they may be closed. This is an aspect of their privacy issues and their need to grow up and be separate from us, and I don't recommend that we push them to talk. We can show them we're aware that life and sexuality are stressful just by making simple comments that show we know that they have challenges, such as realizing that they probably have sexual desires or have people that they like. We need to remember that it is stressful to have a body, especially one with surging hormones. Adolescents face this at a time when they are beginning to take on the stresses of the adult world, and they are uncertain about what the future holds.

CHAPTER 27
CHRONICLE #5: MARRIED WOMEN AND RELATIONSHIP TRIANGLES

I am not proud to say that I have had a relationship with a married woman. I am certainly not alone in this; it seems that the parental issues regarding the incest taboo are so deep and compelling that many people have been in some form of sexual triangle. Triangles are a recreation of the incest taboo because they represent various aspects of feeling separated from our parents. When we are in a triangle, we are often subconsciously trying to break down the barriers and separation we felt from them. When we try to get the unavailable person to love us, it is a recreation of trying to get our parents' love.

The number of people who have been in sexual triangles seems to increase if the culture has a degree of sexual freedom. In my case, that culture was the personal growth movement of the seventies in California, where there was a fairly relaxed attitude about sex and relationships to start with.

I have had a number of powerful relationships, which I felt were a re-creation of my relationship with my mother. This took three basic forms. The first was having relationships with women who were recovering from being hurt by unconscious men. While this is not directly a triangle, it does have the residue of a third person being involved in the relationship. This was a re-creation of my need to be an emotional support to my mother after my parents' divorce. Sometimes this basic energy was present even if it was the woman who had ended her prior relationship. I had a history of trying to be the knight in shining armor who came along to make things better. I did this with a very "New Age" tool-kit, where I proved the depth of my love with spiritual sensitivity.

The second way I re-created my relationship with my mother was by having relationships with women who were thirty-six—the same age my mother was when she was divorced. I have always been attracted to older women, and between the ages of nineteen and twenty-three, I had three significant relationships with women who were thirty-six. This is one way the subconscious works. We can re-create things very literally, and this can be the case with a wide variety of issues, not just our sexuality.

The third way I worked out my mother issues was by having affairs with married women. I had one brief affair and one that was longer and more involved. Whether or not you agree that being in a relationship with someone who is married is a re-creation of parental issues or trying to prove your worth to your parents, it is likely that you can see that an aspect of it is about longing for something that you can't have. I contend that being with someone who is married is one of the most basic ways we re-create our yearning for greater connection in general, and more specifically our yearning for greater connection to our parents. Other ways we can easily re-create these feelings are through long distance relationships and by having relationships with addicts or workaholics. This can be further generalized and understood as an unavailability pattern, which is the tendency to have relationships with people who are unavailable.

Having relationships with people who are unavailable due to marriage, long distance, substance addiction, or work addiction are some of the basic structures where our feelings that our parents were unavailable can be felt or re-created. It is important to note that unavailability can also be emotional. When someone is emotionally unavailable, it has the same triangular feeling as physical triangles. When we are in relationships with people who are not emotionally present, it triggers our fears of abandonment or our vulnerable side, and we are likely to chase them in an attempt to get our needs met.

The relevance of these patterns to creating monogamy is that to create a long-term relationship, we need to resolve, at least to an extent, the patterns and agendas that keep us yearning and seeking connection. The state of seeking keeps us in "chase mode." The result is a failure to connect, just as we are only partly connected if our partner is in another relationship. It's as if when we are "seeking," our real agenda is to "seek but not find." Thus, a key to creating a relationship is to be with and nurture ourselves, and develop a sense of completion with ourselves. We need to feel good enough regardless of our relationship status. To be in a state of yearning tends to perpetuate the pattern of not being with someone.

Earlier in my life, because I faced so many rejections, I had at least partly resolved my abandonment issues, and the releases and insights I received in therapy and breathwork enabled me to become more complete within myself. If I had not created clarity within myself and become better at self-soothing, my abandonment issues would have continued to fuel my needing to be in a relationship, possibly moving from one relationship to the next to prove that I am good enough and worthy.

My next challenge was to resolve a more specific layer, with similar behaviors and consequences that were very central to my self-esteem. This was the need to prove that I was good enough for my mother and that I was better than my father. If not resolved, being in a state of yearning would have led to a continuous state of seeking but not finding. If I were still trying to prove my worth to my parents, I wouldn't be monogamous. I would be out looking for another mother substitute to please, help, or to whom I could prove I was good enough.

Alice was a married woman with whom I had an involved affair where I learned the most about my need to prove that I was good enough. My first contact with Alice was very much like love at first sight. Alice and I met at a workshop where we were both participants. The chemistry between us was explosive, and we began a sexual relationship that weekend but did not make love. Alice returned to her husband and told him about connecting with me and that she wanted an open relationship. Next, Alice, her husband, and I met and negotiated ground-rules about how this open relationship could work. Interestingly, Alice was thirty-six at the time; I was twenty-two.

Alice's husband began another relationship of his own, and I dated other women. One of the ground-rules was that I was supposed to see other women so that my interest wouldn't be so heavily weighted toward Alice, but this was hard for me. Alice and I got more and more serious, and the power of our relationship led to discussions of her leaving her husband. We felt a soul mate connection. At the time, I felt our love was spiritual, divine, and certainly innocent.

At the same time, our psychological training (I was in private practice as a counselor and had been teaching personal growth seminars since I was twenty) pushed us to admit that there were also neurotic issues being acted out. My admission that this beautiful relationship was also about my proving that I was good enough for my mother and better than my father came to a head when I spent an afternoon being confronted by five of my teachers and peers. To confront each other and process what was "off" about each other was commonplace, so the integrity (or lack thereof) of my relationship with Alice was a very appropriate topic of conversation.

We spent what felt like an eternity in a hotel room looking at what the other purposes of my relationship with Alice were. I was partly defensive, citing the divinity of our connection. They insisted that this must also be connected to some of my parental issues and that it simply lacked integrity to be having an affair with a married woman, regardless of whether her husband knew or had consented to our affair. As a teacher of relationship patterns, I had already been looking at these issues, and I was fond of saying that everything is both neurotic and divine. So, they helped me admit what neurotic issues this divine relationship represented.

Mainly I was trying to prove that I was good enough for my mother. This was being played out with Alice because in many ways she desired me more than she desired her husband. Subconsciously this was like my mother telling me that I was better than my father. A second major issue was the need to nurture or care-take Alice, to help her feel better about herself and meet some of her needs that were not being met in her marriage. This was a re-creation of my caretaking my mother after my parents' divorce.

The third big issue, and perhaps the most difficult to admit, was that I had a need to prove I was better than my father. My relationship with Alice exposed a competitive drive I had with my father because it represented an attempt to get my mother to want me more than my father. If I could get Alice to want me more than her husband, it would prove that I was better than my father. It was hard to admit that I was expressing competitive feelings toward my father and Alice's husband. I decided that I needed to let go of these patterns and end the relationship. Alice understood, and we had one very sad but gratitude-filled final date.

I worked on all three of these aspects of the pattern with affirmations. For the "good enough for Mom" issue, I used the following affirmations:

"I proved I am good enough for my mother; I can relax and get my own mate now."

"I proved I am good enough; I can relax now."

"I proved my mother wants me; I can relax now."

For the caretaking issue, I worked with the following:

"I bring only good to people" (therefore I don't have to take care of them).

"It's not my job to take care of women."

"Since my mother takes care of herself, I am safe."

And lastly for the competition issue:
"I proved I am better than my father; I can relax now."
"My presence alone is good enough."

Using the word "proved" in the above affirmations is not very common, but I have found this type of affirmation to be helpful when affirmations are used to let go of compensation issues. They are intended to be similar to telling a lazy person who is not working, "I proved I am divine and deserve to rest; I can get up and get a job now."

While the main key to letting go was to resolve my own issues, it helped me to realize that Alice and her husband were also acting out issues of their own. Alice's issue was centered on her being dissatisfied in her marriage, particularly with regard to her husband's lack of interest in her sexually and spiritually. I filled a gap and helped her feel wanted and desired. She also may have been using me to express anger about her situation to her husband. Her husband's issue seemed to be about being subconsciously relieved that she was getting her needs met elsewhere, and this enabled him to feel less pressured to please her.

Realizing that I was also a pawn in their lives helped me accept that this was part of a larger pattern that was not ideal. It also helped me accept myself and not overly shame myself for my behavior. This kind of acceptance and release of shame made the relationship easier to release. Shaming or making yourself wrong for what you're doing just compounds problems and makes it harder to choose to release unsupportive behaviors.

The main resolution came in two parts: first, from changing my behavior pattern and not seeing Alice; second, by making a firm commitment to myself not to get involved romantically with someone who was in another relationship. I also committed to not having relationships with people who were unavailable either emotionally or due to other circumstances, such as work or physical distance.

Once I ended my involvement with Alice, I hit bottom in my relationships with women. At the time, virtually all of the women to whom I was attracted were in other relationships or were married. If my attraction was strong, it appeared to be connected to their being unhappily married. If my attraction was very strong, it appeared to be because they were unhappily married and thirty-six years old. I knew this because I would discretely inquire about these details with some of the women to whom I found myself attracted. During this period, I could walk down the street and tell you a woman's marital status just by noticing what kind of attraction I felt. My strongest attractions were only to married women, and as I had committed to not having affairs, I felt I would never have another relationship.

I was twenty-three years old, had a wide range of interests, was reasonably desirable physically, and had a promising career—but I felt no hope of ever being attracted to or connecting with anyone who was single. I noticed attractive single women but felt no chemistry.

I spent several months embracing this hopelessness and accepting that I might remain celibate forever. As I worked with these feelings and my affirmations, things gradually shifted. I began dating, and I felt more self-esteem and less abandonment issues in general. My attractions became more varied, and I met Paula three months later. I can still sometimes notice how these variables affect my attractions, and I still have a keen eye for thirty-six-year-old women in general.

Alice and I remain friends to this day. We have talked several times over the past twenty-eight years and had lunch together once. It is interesting to note that there was no sexual chemistry between us when we met. We were both complete with the past and had moved on in our lives.

CHAPTER 28
BIRTH SCRIPTS

A birth script is a compilation of the conclusions about ourselves, our lives, and our relationships, which we carry from our birth and re-create or re-enact throughout our lives. In the section on laws of attraction, I used an example of how the prenatal or birth issues of feeling wanted, feeling wanted as a man or woman, and feeling like a financial burden can affect self-esteem and, therefore, monogamy. In the section on induction patterns, I also mentioned how birth complications can affect relationships and desire patterns. In this chapter and the next, I outline birth scripts or birth experience in a more general way, which will explain their impact on relationship issues as a whole. This, more than any topic in this part of the book, would need a whole book to address in full.

Pre and peri-natal psychology hosts many additional topics, involving the process of delivery and various childbirth practices, which I will not be addressing. I will be focusing on the belief systems that can originate from our birth because they affect relationships the most.

Feeling that we are loved and that we belong in the world is central to self-esteem and feeling worthy in relationships. This all starts with our birth and prenatal experience. How our parents feel toward us in the beginning is central to our psyche. Prior to 1970, the most progressive tenet of psychology was that early childhood experience was at the root of all relationship patterns. Since that time, a flood of research has proven that babies were thinking, feeling, and drawing conclusions about themselves at the time of their birth. Understanding birth and its impact has led to some important insights. It is an extremely vulnerable point in time, and many key identity issues are felt very deeply at our birth. Things like being planned or wanted, being the gender our parents preferred, or financial or emotional burdens all have a huge impact on the self-esteem, guilt, and shame we may carry throughout life. If we tried to look at some of the same issues via family systems theories, the view can become more complicated. Focusing on our birth can give us a simpler description of the issues. At the very least, using the lens of pre- and perinatal psychology gives us an additional point in time to become conscious of and resolve our core relationship issues.

Perhaps breathwork's greatest contribution to psychology is viewing our early life from the perspective of understanding the simple beliefs that originate from our birth and prenatal experience. By understanding the conclusions that various stresses lead babies to draw about themselves, breathworkers have been able to give their clients simple affirmations that cut through and help resolve complex relationship issues.

It is helpful to understand that a baby's early feelings and memories exist before their awareness of language is developed. The feelings are held, but initially words are not attached to them. They are recorded in *preverbal thought*.

As language develops, we attach words that most specifically express the pre-verbal feelings to them. Those words then carry the upsetting feelings. The memories are encoded into language in addition to being stored as preverbal thought in the subconscious mind. This helps explain how affirmations can be effective. Good affirmations pinpoint and trigger the old upset and then specifically help reverse it. The specific words that express how we felt within our old belief systems are important.

In the sections below, it may seem like the issues are generally similar and the variations within each category may seem almost identical. This is true, but the specific subtleties will be important in both contacting the old feelings and releasing them; therefore, the specifics are important. The exact language is important in affirmation work because we want to push (or release) the button precisely.

Breathworkers have found that most people have a wide variety of relationship patterns that are organized around one or two core negatives, which have often been referred to as the *personal law* or, since the mid-eighties, many breathworkers have referred to it as the *personal lie*. We changed the name from "Law" to "Lie" because these beliefs are insecurities, not truths, and people are trained to obey laws. The personal lie is just that, a lie; it was never really true. It's also interesting to note that given our compensation patterns, we have all probably proven our personal lie false many times over. Our personal lie is probably the cause of many negative results, and it is important to change the negative belief and release the feelings associated with it, although another part of the release is to relax and not work so hard to try to prove it wrong.

It may help us better understand how core beliefs affect us if we understand that while low self-esteem is common, and unconsciously anticipating abandonment is common, the specific issues that generate these feelings are unique and vary from individual to individual. Our main self-esteem or monogamy affirmation will probably not be *I love myself, I am a lovable person, and I deserve monogamy.* It will likely be more specific, something like: *I am now wanted, I have the right to be here, I am good enough, I am good enough as a man/woman, I am a contribution/asset, I bring only good to people,* or *I'm legitimate.* All of these are core worthiness issues and affect all aspects of receiving in life and relationships. If we believe these deeper positives, then we will naturally feel worthy of what we want, including monogamy.

While these affirmations may still sound somewhat general, they do address more specific issues that may have originated from birth. Some breathworkers call these core affirmations an *eternal law*, which is a cute name because, just as the personal lie has been the source of a lifetime of relationship upsets, the eternal law can serve as a mantra that will eternally guide you to healthy results. Here's a list of a few major birth scripts and some suggestions, including affirmations/eternal laws, about how to resolve them.

Being unwanted

This, even if our parents got over it quickly and wanted us, seems to result in shame for being alive and results in feeling unworthy. In breathwork, many clients have reported that if they were initially unwanted by one or both of their parents, or by a sibling, it left lasting fears regardless of how their parents responded to them after their birth. It's easy to see how feeling unwanted, if unresolved, is receptive and attractive to physical and emotional abandonment as well as to your partner having affairs or leaving you for another. It can also result in a conquest pattern, where you leave a relationship or don't commit because you need to prove over and over again that you are wanted.

The *affirmations* for this are:

"I am now wanted."

"I have the right to be here."

"I choose to be here" (often out of feeling unwanted people don't want to be here, and this affects their relationships similarly to induction patterns).

"I'm legitimate" (if you were unwanted because of illegitimacy).

"I'm good enough."

I'm good enough is a more general affirmation, but it is often part of the baby's conclusion. The baby might feel, "They don't want me, I must not be good enough."

If it is for the conquest issue, you could do, *"I proved I am wanted; I can relax now."*

Feeling unwanted or not good enough because you were the wrong sex

This is a very common issue, especially for women, because the patriarchal nature of most cultures results in parents often wanting their offspring to be males. The history of farming and ranching has exacerbated this further, but even in white-collar families, it is common. A father once told me that he wanted boys because it increased their chances of success as adults.

Over 60% of my clients report that they feel their parents' generation had a preference about the sex of their unborn child. At minimum, this means thirty percent of the adult population has some feeling of inadequacy associated with their gender. This is a more specific way people may feel unwanted, which creates similar abandonment, rejection, and compensation issues. If a woman does not feel good enough as a woman, it will make it harder for her to feel safe with intimacy or that she deserves monogamy. She may also compensate by having an affair to prove her worth as a woman.

Gender worthiness issues are also common with men who have older brothers. For example, if a couple wanted a boy and a girl, and they had two boys instead, the second boy may have the belief he's not good enough as a man. Also, although patriarchal culture results in more anti-female tendencies, some parents have anti-male tendencies. For example, a woman with a history of abuse at the hands of men may prefer to have girls. Men who feel inadequate because their parents would have preferred that they were girls will be more likely to have affairs to prove their masculinity, or they may attract a non-monogamous partner.

If low self-esteem related to gender is at the core of someone's abandonment or feelings of unworthiness, it can be difficult to identify. It is very threatening to admit that we do not feel good enough as a man or as a woman. If we feel flawed in our sex identity, we will feel hopeless about changing it, and will tend to bury the issue very deeply. This is an area where people tend to compensate greatly. When we compensate for any pattern, we essentially try to prove it wrong by proving the opposite to be the case, which makes the underlying vulnerability even more difficult to admit. Someone who feels unwanted may have collected a lot of evidence to prove they are wanted. They might have a lot of people on a string. (This would apply to the prior section about being unwanted in general, too.)

At a workshop, I once had a participant share that she was a call girl with a waiting list. I immediately hypothesized that her parents wanted a boy. Later in the weekend, when we covered this material, she agreed. These compensation patterns are often played out in business. Many women with this issue take on careers where they feel that they have to compete with men, and they often enjoy being better than men.

To look at the possibility that your parents preferred a child of the opposite sex, first look at their prejudices and their situation. If you're from a farming or ranching family, they probably wanted the first few children to be boys. If your father is from a big city with a white-collar job but is conservative and patriarchal, he probably would have preferred for his first child to be a boy and his second to be a girl. If you have a sibling who is older and of the same sex as you, the chances of your parents having preferred you to be the other sex go up. If you were the second of two boys, your mother probably would have preferred you to be a girl. Even if your parents were split on the issue, I find that you will still carry some of the negatives. Having one parent who wanted you to be the sex you are doesn't erase the imprint of the unworthiness you would have felt from the other.

I also want to note that having a preference on our children's gender is a form of conditional love. Any preference is dysfunctional because it is a form of pressure, where the person with the preference has conditions about what would make us more lovable. These conditions act in a way similar to possession issues. The person with the conditions is not interested in us unconditionally; our identity is being used to help them feel better or more comfortable themselves. Having a sex preference for a child tells the child that they have to do or be something that will make the parent feel better. I consider gender preference to be an early form of parent-child role reversal that is similar to the problems often discussed when family systems theorists problematize a parent's narcissism. This is because they want something from us (a certain gender), and this is contrary to their being there for us. Our sex identity should not be a commodity to help our parents feel better about themselves. Letting go of gender preferences as a society will help us heal the possessive archetypes. Addressing this issue in our lives will help us let go of feeling the pressure and suffocation issues that accompany feeling like a trophy or possession.

Even if our parents did have strong preferences, and we were the sex they preferred, I have often seen it result in similar low self-esteem patterns. In this case, it is as if the child concludes, "If I am only good enough because I am a woman or man, that is way too much pressure and I refuse to cooperate. I'll never be good enough to live up to their expectations." This can result in the core negative, *I refuse to be a woman/man.*

The negative conclusions in this category tend to be as follows: I'm not wanted as a man/woman; I'm not good enough as a man/woman; I'm wrong as a man/woman; there's something wrong with me as a man/woman. All of these are core worthiness issues and affect all aspects of receiving in life and relationships. If we feel unworthy or undeserving, we will be less able to attract what we want or need. We will also be less able to ask for love, intimacy, or monogamy.

The *affirmations* are:

"I am wanted as a man/woman."

"I am good enough as a man/woman."

"I am good enough to be wanted as a man/woman."

"It is right to be a man/woman."

"I am perfect as a man/woman."

"It is perfect to be a man/woman."

"It is good to be a man/woman."

Since you may want to use more than one of these, if not all of them, you can combine them. For example, the affirmation, *"I am wanted and good enough as a man/woman,"* would be a good one to start with. For compensation issues, the affirmation, *"I proved I am good enough as a man/woman; I can relax (and be monogamous) now"* would be helpful.

A footnote to these sex issues is that I do not believe there is a universal connection to feeling unwanted as a man or woman and the issue of homosexuality. I have found the numbers of homosexual men and women who felt not good enough as a man or woman to be about the same as the heterosexual population—about thirty percent. So, I recommend these affirmations to them, but not as a means of changing their sexual orientation. I have heard of teachers in the field of personal growth and relationships who used this perspective to encourage homosexuals to change their sexual orientation, and I am strongly opposed to this. In fact, I have not heard of any psychological theory that adequately explains homosexuality, and I feel that the only place to put our efforts is in dealing with the impact social judgment has on identity and self-esteem. This is similar to, although greater than, the judgment often faced by other minorities, including those getting divorced, home schooling, or having open marriages.

Being a burden

This is another specific reason we might have felt unwelcome in the world. There are a variety of stresses that can be categorized here; the two most basic are feeling like a financial burden and feeling like an emotional burden. It is important to work with them specifically. If we feel like a burden, we will not feel worthy of what we want in relationships, including monogamy.

If your parents felt that they lacked the money to have you, you might have concluded that you were a burden, and the affirmations, *"I am an asset,"* or *"I am a contribution"* are important.

Often the issue is emotional, where one or both of our parents felt they lacked the time or sanity to be able to care for us. The most common reason for this is if our parents already had children or too many young children. Another is if they didn't trust their own emotional state and their ability to be parents. Most parents have some fears like this, but if it was strong and took the form of resentment, then the beliefs about being a burden enter the picture.

Another possibility is that our parents felt that having us interrupted their dreams or careers. If we thought we held a parent back from their life and what was important to them, it would make us feel as if our needs are a burden, and the affirmation, *"Supporting me frees people"* would be appropriate.

Feeling that we are an emotional burden often results in feeling that we do not deserve emotional support, and the negative belief may be felt as, "I'm hard to support." It is also an aspect of feeling that we, or our needs, are not important. The *affirmations* for feeling like an emotional burden are then:

"I'm easy to support."
"I'm a contribution."
"I'm an asset."
"People love to support me."
"I'm important."
"My needs are important."

To attract or allow intimacy, we need to feel that our energy is good. Feeling like a burden can cause any number of self-esteem problems. We might feel unworthy of what we want, and we might be prone to settling for less than what we want.

Feeling not good enough

I find the belief "I'm not good enough" to be the most common personal lie. This is in part because it most accurately expresses the way we naturally strive to be a good person. Worrying about the opposite—that is, not being good enough—then becomes a most universal fear. It is as if when in doubt we work to protect ourselves by becoming as good as possible. In the case of our birth, I find that if there weren't more specific stresses, such as those already mentioned, upon which to focus, the mind worries about simply being good enough. Just as the most basic human need is to feel loved and that we belong, the most basic way we fear we might not deserve love is to fear that we are not enough or are not good enough.

This was the case with my birth. When I was being carried away from my mother, I felt rejected by her, and I concluded that I must not be good enough. The more specific issues about my being wanted and planned and them wanting a boy were not at issue, so my survival instincts were to worry about not being good enough.

People with the personal lie "I'm not good enough" often don't really need to connect it to their birth. It seems to be the personal lie of people without much unresolved on the birth level whose most basic stresses come from their parents' general pressure or expectations for them to succeed or be a good person. In this case, birth scripts don't need to be brought into the picture, but using the affirmation, *"I'm good enough"* can help work through parental issues in general.

Feeling "not good enough" creates basic rejection feelings on one hand, and on the other, it results in the most general compensation patterns. It affects relationships and monogamy by causing people to stay out of relationships or by attracting abandonment. It might also generate conquest patterns, where a person might always be on the hunt to find someone who will then prove they are good enough.

The *affirmation* for this is as follows:

"I'm good enough."

Note: If you have the belief "I'm not good enough," and you need this affirmation, you will be tempted to project that the affirmation isn't good enough. The affirmation is good enough! This is the best place to explain the importance of not overcompensating when you create affirmations. For example, the affirmations *"I'm the best"* or *"I'm the greatest"* are not believable to the subconscious and therefore do not work.

Other affirmations that work and fit this category are:
"I'm enough."
"I'm more than enough."
"I've proved I'm good enough; I can relax now."

Feeling that you are bad

The personal lie "I'm bad" is similar to "I'm not good enough" but is more negative and most commonly seems to be the result of how religious ethics can compound the worry of not being good enough. If we grow up worrying about not being good enough, and our environment has an emphasis on good and bad, right and wrong, and good and evil, the language "I'm bad" can easily become our core insecurity.

The belief "I'm bad" can also be more connected to birth scripts than the belief "I'm not good enough" because it can be a conclusion that some people draw as part of the birth stresses of feeling unwanted or a burden, and feeling bad if we caused our mother pain. These conclusions might be felt as "They don't want me; I must be bad" or "I'm a burden; I must be bad" or "I hurt her; I must be bad." Feeling bad can create the same unworthiness or compensation issues as any core negative, but it is also worth noting how this could fuel shame-based beliefs about sex and sexuality. People who feel bad are certainly likely to feel their desires are bad, and they may feel bad for wanting sex. It is a form of compensation when some people get more sexually aroused if they are told that they are bad.

The *affirmation* is:

"I'm good."

Affirmations about innocence are also valuable, for example:

"I'm an innocent and good child of God; all of my desires are holy, and they always have been."

Many people will also find value in connecting this to the other issues. For example, by using affirmations like:

"Since I'm good, I am now wanted."

"I am good; I have the right to be here."

Or one of my favorites:

"I've proved I'm good; I can relax now."

There is something wrong with me

The belief "there is something wrong with me" is similar to the beliefs "I'm not good enough" and "I'm bad" but is more specific and is usually influenced by some concern about our health or imperfections surrounding our birth. The concern could be that our parents feared birth defects or that there actually was a birth defect or health concern. I find that even if the problem was insignificant—for example, if we came out and our ear was folded or our head misshapen from the birth canal—and a parent or medical personnel responded with any feeling of there being something wrong, that we would take this on as, "Oh no, there's something wrong with me." If we have this belief, we tend to have more adamant right/wrong issues in our relationships and communications. Instead of working to prove that we are good enough, we will be trying to prove that we are not wrong. At times, we will appear to be trying to prove we are right. This results in increased defensiveness and arguing with couples.

It is worth noting that defensiveness is a form of compensation, and that any of these core negatives can fuel communication problems. Just as these negative beliefs might motivate us to have affairs to prove our worth or desirability, they can also make us fear criticism, and we may be unnecessarily defensive because of the fear of being wrong. This creates arguments where we are trying to prove that we are right. All of the negatives I've mentioned thus far result in defensiveness. For example, if we are trying to prove we are good enough or wanted, we will also be unnecessarily defensive.

This is a good time to repeat that the language of affirmations needs to be specific. Just because we act out or compensate for the negatives in similar ways, the beliefs that fuel the behaviors differ and need to be addressed specifically. This issue of feeling that there is something wrong with me might feel almost identical to "I'm not good enough," but the affirmation would be *"I'm perfect the way I am"* or *"I'm perfect exactly the way I am."* The difference between the two affirmations is that here the word "perfect" should do a better job of triggering and resolving the old feelings of being wrong or imperfect.

People who fear that there is something wrong with them seem to have perfectionist parents, or at least they perceive them to be perfectionists. Their right/wrong issues have a tone of trying to prove their innocence to their parents or other authorities. The affirmation, *"I proved there is nothing wrong with me; I can relax now"* may therefore be helpful. This could help to let go of defensiveness and righteousness in relationships.

People with this issue also tend to extend this fear into their behavior and fear that they did the wrong thing. They might feel that their partner had an affair because they said or did the wrong thing. Here the affirmations, *"I always do the right thing"* and *"Everything I do is right,"* will help us remember that we can't cause another person's behavior, and any shortcomings of ours cannot cause another person to do anything unless they also have their own issues at play.

Feeling rejected if you were separated from your mother

Being separated from our mother after our birth leads to a variety of feelings of rejection. Separation after birth, even if only for a short time so that the medical staff could clean us, weigh us, and take blood tests can result in various feelings of abandonment. A gentle childbirth perspective suggests that when there is not a serious health concern, all of these things can wait or be done while the newborn is with the mother or non-birthing parent. Many of us were separated from our parents for hours or may have spent days in the hospital nursery, and we only saw our mother when we were given feedings.

Separation is a more general experience than those listed above, but I'm giving it its own section because it also results in many of the issues above. Being separated from our mothers at birth can result in feelings of inadequacy and abandonment even if the overall family dynamics don't cater to any of the negatives I've mentioned. For example, being separated from our mothers at birth can make someone who was wanted and planned feel unwanted. It is not just our experience that leads to these core negative beliefs but also the conclusions we each draw that are most valuable to look at. Two babies could have the same experience and conclude two different things. This is especially true for something more general, like being removed from our mother. One person might conclude, "Oh, she must not want me." Another might conclude, "I must not be good enough," and another might think it was because, "There is something wrong with me."

This is also the case with the other stresses listed in the previous sections. Two people could have a similar experience, such as feeling unwanted or that they were a burden financially, and conclude different things. All of these ideas need to be specifically applied on a case-by-case basis. On the other hand, a specific trauma usually results in a specific conclusion, and the specific affirmation will be a key to resolving the issue even if it feels like there are more feelings connected to it. For example, virtually every woman whose parents wanted them to be a boy will benefit from using the affirmations, *"I am good enough as a woman,"* or *"I am now wanted as a woman."*

CHAPTER 29
THE INFANT GUILT SYNDROME:
CAUSING OUR MOTHERS PAIN

I am separating this issue from the other birth issues and giving it its own chapter because of its broad and far-reaching affect on monogamy. The belief that "We cause pain" is the most universal negative that comes out of the physical act of childbirth. Delivering a baby hurts: mothers fear it, it is bloody, they are often given anesthesia to numb the pain, and they may tear or be given an episiotomy that bleeds and has to be stitched back up. A caesarean section is surgery.

No matter how gentle or natural our birth, one thing we all have in common is that we hurt our mothers. If our delivery was difficult or if our mother had a strong fear of the pain of childbirth, then this issue might have become our core negative. Especially if the more basic loving and belonging issues were okay, then causing pain may have been the key stress surrounding our delivery. We tend to focus on whatever is our "weak link," and if causing our mother pain was ours, we may have focused on it and worried about it since.

This was the case with me. I was wanted and planned, had an older sister, and my parents wanted a boy. But my mother had a difficult twenty-four-hour labor with my sister, and she was afraid to give birth to me. My mother's medical needs were being cared for by an HMO (yes, we had HMO's in 1958), and she was worried about who the doctor on call would be when she delivered. She got the doctor she least wanted—a cold man who was an ex-military doctor.

During the initial stages of labor, she expressed her fear of pain to him and he said, "Don't worry, honey; if you could remember the pain from the first child, you wouldn't be here now."

By many standards, my birth was relatively easy, but my memory of it, in addition to the above, is that after I came out they gave my mother gas so she could rest and they could more easily sew up her episiotomy. As I was being carried away, I could see and feel her drifting away, and I felt that she didn't want me because I had hurt her. I have these memories partly from breathwork and partly from my mother's stories.

So in my case I had two personal lies. Both originated from the feeling of separation and abandonment I felt as I was being separated from my mother at birth. It is common for people to have more than one personal lie. If you feel you do, it is important to work with each one and not use working with one to avoid working with the others.

In chronicle #1, I wrote about how my father's adultery had made me fear that I would hurt women and encouraged me to nurture people instead. I said a monogamous psychotherapist was born. Here these same comments apply—a nurturer was born. This example also nicely illustrates the value of using multiple lenses to work with the same issue. I have found that this is how life works:

whatever our core issue is, it was probably played out within multiple spheres of influence. My need to be nurturing and not hurt people originates at my birth and within my parents' divorce. Having multiple lenses in which to see this gives me more ability to see and resolve the issue.

It is also interesting to note that I have found that many obstetricians have similar stories about hurting their mother. I had a student who was an obstetrician and also specialized in gentle birth. At one of the workshops he attended, I was trying to help him connect with the origin of his caretaking issues, and he was having a hard time seeing the connection to his birth. As I tried to summarize what I had been saying to him, I asked, "Well, did you hurt your mother when you were born?" To which he replied, "Yes, I split her from stem to stern." (That's crude talk for ripping the mother's vagina to where it connects with her anus.) The whole group laughed, partly in horror and partly because he still couldn't see how this was an aspect of his desire to be an obstetrician and provide support in gentle childbirth.

A breathworker named Kyle Os discovered this issue of feeling ashamed because we hurt our mothers in the '70s and later labeled it the Infant Guilt Syndrome. It was quite a revelation at the time to discover that it was this level of old guilt that ran people's lives. In spite of this revelation, the topic was still so deep and obtuse that it took them days to come up with the affirmation. It was as if they hadn't watched Perry Mason enough to be able to remember that the opposite of guilt is innocence, and a basic affirmation would be, *"I'm innocent."*

 The infant guilt syndrome offers a substantial explanation of what needs to be resolved in order to feel that we are good and worthy people. Since the '80s, the topic of shame has become central in many psychological circles, and it's important to note that shame may be a better term for what breathworkers initially called guilt. Guilt is feeling that we did something wrong, and shame is feeling that our existence is bad or wrong. Feeling that we did something wrong by hurting our mother creates shame for being alive because it is as if we feel that our existence in the world inevitably hurts others.

A belief that corresponds to "I cause pain" is "People hurt me." These beliefs are some of the biggest, if not *the* biggest, issues behind how we can attract pain in relationships or be unconsciously motivated to hurt others. Our sexuality is an area where we have the propensity to betray and hurt each other, but it can help if we realize that the sexual issues are often just a way to act out unconscious beliefs. If someone is causing a partner pain by being abusive, having an affair, or by leaving the relationship, they may be acting out the belief that they cause pain, and the person being hurt may also be manifesting the belief that people hurt me.

It is valuable to realize that there is a connection between birth, pain, and sex. Our whole existence is affected by the connection between sex, childbirth, and pain. Sex can lead to birth, which causes pain. The result is that we have unconscious issues in which we expect sex to hurt and cause us pain (sometimes physically). With this unconscious expectation for sex to cause pain, we are driven to act it out. Having affairs becomes one of the easiest ways to hurt the ones we love.

Both men and women experience both sides of the issue, one where we fear hurting others and the other, where we fear being hurt. However, because women are the ones who physically give birth and have pain in childbirth, this issue makes women more susceptible to expecting to be hurt via their sexuality. The idea that sex can lead to pain is very real to a woman. For a man, the idea that if he gets a woman pregnant he will hurt her is equally real. I feel that this explains the notion that women are more often in the role of feeling that their sexuality caused them pain, and men are more often in the role of feeling that their sexuality has hurt someone they love.

The fear of physical pain from childbirth has been translated into the emotional arenas by the subconscious. Note that I am only addressing childbirth here and haven't even discussed the large and very real issue of how patriarchy has caused women pain.

Being aware of this has increased my respect for how deeply sexual issues impact us, and how easy it is to be hurt following the vulnerability of sexual intimacy. It is important to be committed to not hurting others with our sexuality. There are two issues to resolve. The first is to commit to not hurting people, and the second is not to buy into the illusion that we make people hurt. We can act responsibly and respectfully without projecting our mother's pain or the pain of childbirth on to others. As a man, I try to respect that if I make love to a woman, it may lead to a depth of love where she (as well as me) is likely to become vulnerable to being hurt. Simultaneously, I try to treat her as a powerful, capable woman who can take care of herself. This is the same thing I want from women. We all need sensitivity and respect without condescension.

It also helps to work through guilt and shame if we realize that they are vast and almost vague feelings. Guilt and shame are not specific emotions; they are conditions within which we will experience a variety of feelings. The condition is thinking or feeling that our existence is bad or wrong. This includes a whole host of feelings, such as anger, fear, and sadness.

Discovering our innocence is a key to healing the infant guilt syndrome. Innocence is an essence of our core, which can most easily be felt in the absence of guilt and shame. Innocence is a nebulous quality primarily because it is the opposite of shame, and shame is an unconscious and all encompassing context in which we live our lives. It is as if feeling guilty and ashamed for being alive is so basic to our thought process that the opposite feeling is intangible. Innocence is also a nebulous quality in our lives because we are used to earning our worthiness through performance. We work hard in order to justify our existence, or "earn our living." Being innocent is an aspect of feeling that we deserve love, health, and money just for being alive. This notion is very vague in the presence of feeling we have to earn our existence. Feeling that we need to earn our existence is often acted out in relationships and in work, as if we feel it is what we do that makes us worthy. Innocence does not need to be earned; it is something we are, just for being alive.

Shame and unworthiness cause a wide range of relationship problems. Shame is a condition that is receptive or attractive to loss or abandonment in the same way negative beliefs are. Also, if we feel guilty or ashamed, we will feel that we are a bad influence on others or that our desires are wrong. This is the basis for commitment phobia. People actually stay away from relationships in an unconscious effort to protect others from themselves as if they are a toxic influence. Shame also affects desire in general. It is simply too scary to want something if we feel unworthy of it. This affects everything, from committing to our life's purpose, to being able to pursue relationships, to having the strength to want within intimate relationships. Desire is a natural impulse that shines brightly when we feel innocent.

A key to creating innocence is to develop an experience of our worthiness at a being level. Innocence is experienced if we connect with life unconditionally without earning it. This is done when we experience the simpler nature of ourselves and of life. *Being* oriented activities, such as meditation, hiking, bathing, sleeping, sunbathing, playing, and making love, are good activities on which to focus in order to develop innocence, but be careful not to *do* them. It's a contradiction to *do* things to create *being*. Innocence will actually be the experience of being that exists within any activity. If we work at meditation, we are turning it into a *doing* oriented activity. Activities with a slower pace, such as meditation, allow more room within which to experience innocence and being. Ultimately, *being* is a quality of being present that can be felt within any activity. We could be on the floor of the stock exchange and within it all, be so connected to our joy for our self and for life that we are in a profound state of being and innocence.

The most basic *affirmations* for this pattern are:
"*I bring only good to people.*"
"*My aliveness adds to the aliveness of others.*"

Other variations that might be helpful are:
"*I forgive myself for thinking I could hurt people.*"
"*I've proved I bring only good to people; I can relax now.*"

201

*"I am an innocent child of God; all of my desires are holy,
and they always have been."*
"I'm innocent."

The infant guilt syndrome is also a major aspect of why we don't speak up about our sexual needs and instead choose to play it safe and try to be nurturing rather than confront relationship problems. Guilt and shame result in insecurity and make us doubt the validity of what we feel or need. When we don't speak up, we are more likely to look elsewhere for love, as it can be easier to move to a new person. The excitement of a new relationship may also make us feel like we are getting more of what we need without the stress of having to ask for it or address old relationship issues. Innocence is part of being strong enough to confront problems and speak up about our needs.

There are other birth and family categories into which core negative beliefs can fit, but these cover the central birth scripts of at least 90% of the population. This is not intended to say that our birth experience is the only core issue of our early childhood. Birth is a powerful point in time, and the experiences there can be easily simplified. I, and others in the field of pre and peri-natal psychology, find that this simplistic view provides a helpful window into more complex feelings. Just as I added a section on being separated from our mothers, I could also add a section on breast-feeding, circumcision, birth complications, and a whole range of family and parental issues. But, for the purposes of this book, I think one of the many affirmations discussed will help you feel either able to commit to monogamy or worthy and deserving of a monogamous partner.

If the categories seem too simplistic to you, I suggest that our needs are simple. We need to feel that we are loved and that we belong. Given this and the basic possibilities of how we could feel unloved or invalidated at birth, these affirmations and categories cover most of the negative beliefs I find in my practice.

It is important to note that even though two people share the same belief and the same set of affirmations, they may not be resolving the same set of experiences. The ways in which their issues have been acted out within their family and beyond will vary. The affirmations cut to the core, but everyone's core has different layers that surround it. The same affirmation will therefore help two different people work through different feelings and patterns. Affirmations are just one tool of consciousness that can be used, and each individual will get different benefits from various tools, depending on their issues and their styles. Affirmations are by no means a fix or the only tools I teach. I like them because they distill complex issues down to a core, and the affirmation gives a new direction upon which to focus as additional tools are used to choose and create new states of being. Being conscious of the old negatives and having affirmations that help focus on new directions is a powerful aspect of learning to choose new relationship behaviors.

Any time we have a result that is lacking in our life—for example, a partner who is having an affair—we are going to feel hit by it in our weakest link. Our personal lie is a clear description of our weakest self-esteem link. It is the wording of how we take things personally. If someone had

203

the belief, "I'm not good enough" and their partner had an affair, they would interpret it as, "I must not be good enough." Someone with the personal lie, "I'm not good enough as a woman" would interpret their partner having an affair as, "I must not be good enough as a woman." Knowing this gives us greater consciousness about how to recover our self-esteem and how to request a monogamous relationship.

In the example of feeling not good enough as a woman, if she realized that she *is* good enough as a woman, it will give her more strength with which to ask for a monogamous relationship. Metaphysically, with the increased self-esteem of strongly believing she is good enough as a woman, she will be more likely to attract her desired results.

CHAPTER 30
PATRIARCHY, MATRIARCHY, AND MONOGAMY

The influences of patriarchal and matriarchal cultures can affect monogamy both positively and negatively. My favorite definition of culture is "the rules and norms that govern appropriate behavior." A simplistic view suggests that patriarchy has had a negative impact on monogamy because it results in inequitable rules for men and women. The definitions of patriarchy include the father being the head of the family; or, a system that is governed by men. More importantly, patriarchy includes the belief that men are superior to women.

In some patriarchal cultures, this notion has led to the idea that men deserve the privilege of having control over relationships, including the privilege of having multiple partners, a mistress, or affairs. This is the most basic issue to address within this cultural arena, but the idea of matriarchal influences (the superiority of women) needs to be included as well.

Most of us have patriarchy deeply rooted in both our family system, our cultural roots, and perhaps even in our genes. We have many issues going on simultaneously, but one of them is the usually subconscious belief that men are superior and therefore deserve more. This belief is so unconscious and prevalent that we don't even know we are operating from it. It is as if we have a skewed understanding of fairness between men and women and are under the illusion that men are receiving 50% of the resources when in actuality they are receiving more. Patriarchy also tends to elevate women in certain instances; for example, we may feel they deserve to be compensated for all the pain they have endured at the hands of men.

It helps us understand the effect matriarchy and patriarchy have on monogamy and affairs if we take this idea away from the men vs. women approach and instead look at the notion of control, power, and privilege. If someone is having an affair, it will often be rooted in some notion of control or superiority. The person having the affair has put her or himself in a "one up" position. They are acting as if they are entitled to have two partners. In earlier chapters, I explained that much of what drives someone to have an affair are feelings of inadequacy or inferiority. Here we look at how feelings of superiority can fuel infidelity and how it requires some feelings of dominance or righteousness for the average person to justify having an additional partner.

On one hand, most of us were raised to feel that it is bad to have an affair. Thus, it is against our culture or our inner rules. But, if another (perhaps subconscious) aspect of our cultural rules is that men are superior, then we might subconsciously think they deserve more from life than women do. In this elevated status, we could subconsciously be expecting or encouraging men to have affairs. We may still think it is bad for men to have multiple partners, but if they do, we are also more likely to look away or accept it.

From the perspective of biology or "nature," as discussed earlier, this would be because we expect men to be unable to control their sex drive. From the perspective of "patriarchy," it would be because we subconsciously feel it is okay since men are superior and entitled to do so. Patriarchy can also be an aspect of a heterosexual woman justifying an affair. She might feel that "since he's dominated or abused me, I deserve the love and nurturing my lover brings me."

Most people come from a culture with patriarchal messages. The notion of male supremacy can be expressed subtly and unconsciously, or it can be obvious. Some readers, like myself, have had strong matriarchal influences (the belief that women are superior to men), but truthfully I have usually found people's matriarchal influences to be secondary to patriarchy. Ultimately, we can work with both influences without worrying which is dominant.

There are two basic ways to react to any rule or norm: to conform/follow it or rebel/disown it. This is quite similar to how we adopt our families' primary self or disown it. In the area of patriarchy, both men and women have adopted some attitudes where we feel superior or inferior, and others where we angrily fight it or resent its pressure. So men then have two issues: one is the tendency to feel superior and justified in having multiple partners, or secondly their superiority obligates them to be good, true, and monogamous. Sometimes the second issue even fuels affairs because men resent the pressure and want to sabotage their success in a partnership as if to dethrone themselves.

The effect of patriarchy on women could be viewed as creating subservience where women are more likely than men to tolerate a male partner having other lovers than vise versa. But, as I alluded to above, patriarchal roots could influence a woman to have multiple partners. This would be an aspect of rebellion where the abuse she has endured from men makes her feel entitled to have another lover. She might feel that with all that she has been through, she deserves the nurturing she might receive outside of her partnership. Sometimes a woman's entitlement comes from her finally rejecting the oppression of being in the subservient position.

I am not suggesting that all affairs or rebellions are bad. Bluntly put, I would prefer to see women rebel from the abuses of patriarchy in any way they can, and would prefer to see someone leave an abusive partnership in any way they can. In this context, the rebellion factor of having another lover is giving the individual much needed strength to break free from oppression. Note that when we view world history, we rarely criticize the means that revolutionaries use to create democracy.

Matriarchal influences are harder to view because, as I said, they exist within the shadow of patriarchy and tend to be a secondary belief. For those who do feel women are superior to men, then the opposite of my prior statements would be the case—man or woman, they could expect women to have affairs. It is not uncommon to have two opposing beliefs, effectively being pulled in two different directions. This is increasingly evident in our "male bashing" humor, where we put down men and elevate women. The solution is to work to resolve each belief independently. Simply put, we have part of us that feels men are superior and part of us that feels women are superior.

This is the case with myself. I was born in 1958 in a patriarchal, white, upper middle class neighborhood in the United States. But my father was an alcoholic who had affairs that devastated my mother. My mother's victim status combined with my primary residence being with my mother and older sister led to some aspects of matriarchy. I had, as I said earlier in this book, a strong feeling that it was important not to hurt women. I also felt subjugated by my mother and sister, and my vulnerable child felt that women were more important than I was. I also grew to have profound respect for the efforts of childrearing, working women, and working mothers.

In my practice, I have seen many men with similar stories. I find that the stronger a man's female role models were growing up, the more sensitive he is likely to be toward women. This variable is known quite clearly within popular psychology—most heterosexual women know to inquire about how a man feels about his mother early in the relationship!

These matriarchal influences have been an aspect of how I have been comfortable being subservient to women or have placed myself in a one down position, where their needs were more important than my own. It would be valid to say that this was one aspect of my divorce—that I needed to rebel and break away from the subservience and its related symptoms, which I had created in part because of my matriarchal or female dominated roots.

My general feeling is that having matriarchal influences can be helpful because the advancement of the status of women is essential to equality on this planet. The same is true of race, class, and sexual orientation. For true equality to exist, we need to understand the various ways we put each other "one-up" or "one-down" and remember that differences are not equality issues. Differences like childbirth and physical strength make us different but not unequal. Equality is in everyone's interest, including the dominant groups, because when we're one-up, it means we could be one-down someday. It is also very painful when someone we love is "below" us. Our unconditional love wants our beloved to be our equal.

Male readers, notice how upset you would be if your mother, sister, or female partner were to be abused in a personal or work situation, or if they were not able to make equal wages for equal work as men. Seeing this outrage will help you love the women in your life more unconditionally. It will help you let go of inequalities in your relationship at home and do more housework and parenting.

Matriarchal cultures have existed in the recent past, although they have been far less common. When a society is primarily matriarchal, it also results in women having some privileges over men. When women hold power over men—for example, in farming or gathering societies where they do most of the work—men tend to work to regain power by trying to assume an important role even if that role is in fantasy only. For instance, hunting and animal flesh have been given elevated status in some primitive societies where it is not needed because the women's gathering activities were sufficient for sustenance. Men then hunted to create importance, even though their hunting activities in some cases only provided a small percentage of the food source. It is also worth noting that the power of childbirth has elevated and confused women's status in many cultures. I think a simple view of this is that it has given them power but that men have then competed and tried to take back that power by putting women down.

I feel it is critical that couples identify and resolve inequities regardless of the basis of them. Inequities are a source of frustration that result in all kinds of communication and sexual issues. As a counselor, I have often felt that if I only helped a couple see this kind of hierarchy, I would help them with many other issues. For example, when one person feels one-down, they will feel defensive and compensate by trying to elevate themselves, often by putting the other down. Negative communication frequently escalates in relationships, and a solution is to establish a deeper sense of equality.

Another relevance of patriarchy and matriarchy to monogamy is to note how instinctual it is for both genders to need status and power. It is quite common to seek an elevated status in order to justify getting what we want or need. In our present society, issues of power and money create a hierarchy where one individual might use their status to justify their right to have an affair or have their needs be primary. This anthropological conversation serves to expand our sense that any form of being one-up is hazardous to a true partnership and therefore to monogamy.

CHAPTER 31
PRIVILEGE, POWER, AND ENTITLEMENT

Sometimes it is important to take this discussion beyond whether our relationships are patriarchal and look at the issues of power, privilege, and entitlement, which are not necessarily based on gender. Relationships have their own spoken and unspoken rules that govern appropriate behavior. In this way, relationships have their own cultures, and someone's entitlement can be elevated for a variety of reasons beyond gender. We can elevate our partner's or our own entitlement because of education, financial success or superiority, prestigious family background, or other accomplishments. We might elevate our partner's or our own status because we (or they) gave birth. People's status can also be subconsciously elevated to compensate them for past pain. For example, do you feel you "owe" your partner because their life has been harder or because they have made your life easier?

To work with this issue means being committed to equality and to eliminating all power imbalances— including the patriarchal ones in our subconscious. This means not only learning to honor each person's contribution and to let go of the illusions of superiority but also to be diligent at uncovering the subtle and insidious ways that superiority comes out. The first step is to get out of denial and accept that we have all had some influences that led us to believe that we are superior. Understanding these influences enables us to move forward more consciously and not act on these beliefs. Patriarchy takes subtle forms. Some of the most common include listening to men more than women; believing that rational thought is more important than feelings and intuition; and that working for money is more valuable than parenting or homemaking.

When I counsel heterosexual couples, I often feel that my most important job is to help them confront these kinds of hierarchies. Other therapists are working with this also, and the notion of anti-patriarchal counseling is expanding.

If we attribute a sense of superiority to something, it often results in a condescending communication. It is demeaning for us to act as if we are better than others are. For instance, in a one-income household, it is demeaning for the wage earner to act as though they are more important because they bring home a paycheck. That behavior is hurtful for the homemaker. Most couples that have addressed this consciously have come to accept that the homemaker's job is the harder of the two. Being attentive to children and running a household can require more of a homemaker than many jobs do. It requires more multitasking and has more pressure than many workplaces. Work outside of the home is usually simpler because it requires one task at a time, with less interruption. Even upper level management jobs can be easier than homemaking.

My view of the new archetype of partnership is that if two people are together, it is an expression of equality. If they like spending time together, it illustrates that they are both receiving something and are therefore equals. One might be richer, funnier, more educated, or more attractive, but their partner must have something of equal value they are offering. I believe this is a simple and spiritual issue; if people were not spiritual equals, they wouldn't be together. It is only fear that leads someone to want to use their strengths to make them one-up. So, another solution is the simple act of acknowledgment. Acknowledging our partner will remind us to express our equality instead of our fear. Acknowledging them elevates them, and they deserve that. We need not fear being one-down.

CHAPTER 32
NARCISSISM

Narcissism is often an overused term, but it does give some important reminders about why people have more than one lover. The term narcissism comes from a Greek myth in which a young man named Narcissus was obsessed with looking at his own reflection in a lake. The popular use of the term is similar. We are narcissistic when we use our life and relationships to validate our image of ourselves. If the purpose of a relationship is to make us feel better about ourselves, then it is narcissistic. If we have a possession, the purpose of which is to validate our image, then we have a narcissistic relationship to that possession. If we focus on our children's successes so we will feel like better parents, instead of focusing on supporting their image of themselves, then we are narcissistic as parents.

This is an issue for almost everyone and a valuable context in which to view our psychological growth. The healthier we become, the more our feelings of worth are generated from the inside and our relationship with ourselves, and the less they come from outside sources.

The term narcissism is also used to describe a personality disorder that is addressed in abnormal psychology. Here, a client with severe narcissism issues may be defined as having Narcissistic Personality Disorder. It is helpful to accept that everyone has narcissistic issues that do not need to be compared to this disorder. Virtually everyone has some unresolved childhood issues where their identity was not validated in a positive way, and they then tend to seek their identity from the external world and use their relationships to validate their self-image. On the other hand, narcissism can be an overused and simplistic term. It doesn't really help if we sit around calling each other narcissistic. It is more productive if we work with our issues beyond the labels. We all need to identify how we use relationships to feel good about ourselves and reflect our image of ourselves back to us.

Narcissism does not just give motivation to have multiple lovers. It could also be a superficial motivation for monogamy. Someone who is very loyal and monogamous could be doing so to prove their goodness to the world and not because it is what they really want. In the end, conscious choice is the key. Understanding the issues of identity and image will help you choose consciously. Both monogamy and non-monogamy are choices that will be more pure if we act on them for ourselves, instead of to validate how we look to the outside world.

CHAPTER 33
THE MYTH OF THE FREE SPIRIT

I believe that freedom is an essential human need. It is a life affirming quality, like love, that when focused on creates greater purpose and success. Freedom is always a positive thing, and the lack of it always causes problems. That said, there are a variety of less healthy reasons that people are compelled to seek what they perceive to be freedom. These tend to create a view where committed relationships are seen as stifling or oppressive. The myth of the free spirit is the common and sometimes conscious notion that relationships restrict freedom and to be fully free in life one needs to be a free spirit who is not "trapped" in a relationship. I view this as a myth and not a reality because from another perspective, being settled and present in a relationship creates a state in which we are actually more able to expand and be free.

The process of looking for a relationship actually narrows our focus, and our energy is less free. If we experience relationships as stifling or oppressive, this stems from issues in our past, such as growing up with parents who were not happy together or were in abusive or suppressed relationships. Growing up while witnessing the things our parents lost by staying together tends to leave people in a mode of seeking freedom or unfulfilled dreams by moving on to the next person (or job, city, or thing) and then the next, and then the next, etc.

Breathworkers and others in the field of pre and peri-natal psychology have offered some deep insights into the issues of freedom and our ability to be fully intimate while in relationships. Relationships often subconsciously represent the womb, and our comfort or discomfort being in a relationship parallels how we felt when we were inside our mother. The question to tune into here is what was the general environment of our mother's womb? Was it intimate and nourishing? If so, we will likely feel good and supported being in a relationship. If the womb was a stressful place, then we will likely have subconscious feelings that we need to get "out" of relationships. Given that most core relationship issues repeat themselves in multiple ways, someone who felt suffocated or unsupported in the womb would likely feel that later in childhood. So, while the same kinds of questions should be asked about our family life, I have found the pre-natal level of looking at the womb experience to be especially helpful. It also serves as a powerful early metaphor of the family experience.

There are numerous stresses that can make the womb environment uncomfortable. The biggest ones are feeling unloved and unwanted. If we were unwanted, unplanned, a financial burden, or not the sex our parents preferred, it might have made us feel insecure about being alive in general, as already noted. Within the womb environment, it would also influence our ability to feel safe while in an intimate relationship later in life. If our mother was experiencing stress in life in general or with a primary partner, was lacking a primary relationship, or was in an abusive relationship, then this stress would impact us, too. This area even includes things like the stress of moving, especially if it results in our mother losing her support system.

Another important area is our mother's own emotional state. If she were afraid to give birth, we would have felt it. If she smoked cigarettes, it would have increased our physical and emotional stress or given us the feeling that relationships are toxic. (There is evidence to suggest that a baby's heart rate increases when its mother smokes, or even when the mother thinks of having a cigarette.)

One thing that many, many people have felt to some degree is a desire to get out of the womb to get free of stress or negativity. But also note that we all needed to get "out" at some point. If you were still inside your mother, you would both be dead! There is an inevitable stage of growth where we need to leave the womb. Many people have recalled feeling that the womb became increasingly claustrophobic. I have found this to be an issue for virtually everyone to some degree, and as a result, we all have some impulses to move away or out of a relationship. Noticing this can help us stay in a relationship when it is nourishing us. The tendency to project that a relationship is a womb that we need to leave to be free can be viewed as the belief that we need to "get out of here" to survive or be free. The affirmations for this are: *"It's safe to be here," "Relationships add to my freedom,"* and *"The universe is my womb."*

Most people have the opposite pull as well, which is the desire to return to the womb. Ideally, the womb is a nurturing environment where we feel intimate and safe. If this were the case, then we would likely feel the desire to

219

create relationships that re-create this closeness. If our womb experience was basically good and nurturing, then was followed by a birth experience that was more uncomfortable, we would have a primary drive to remain in relationships or any environment (organization, job, city, house, etc.) that could subconsciously represent the womb. This means that we fear leaving relationships because of our fear of birth. This is particularly important if we feel we have strong dependency patterns or are in a relationship that we want to leave but are afraid to. The main point here is that to be genuinely free, we need to be comfortable with the idea of leaving, as well as with staying. Most people will also receive benefit from realizing that it is safe to leave, and I recommend the affirmation, *"It is safe to leave,"* in addition to those above about it being safe to stay.

Another insight that breathworkers have added to this is that the feelings of wanting to get out of here (or the womb) result in the desire to get out of the body and away from the stress of life. The desire to get out of this life can also be driven by the opposing womb issue of wanting to get back into the womb. Often death is subconsciously viewed as a womb-like environment where we will be completely connected to an afterlife or to our loved ones. The desire to die can also be a misguided attempt to get away from the stress of life, which we first felt during the pain or alienation of our birth. Death becomes the relief point where we might be able to get away from the stress of life and return to the nourishment we felt in the womb. Death or relationships can be equally viewed as an all encompassing, nurturing environment, like having "24 hour womb service."

Breathworkers have referred to the general depressive, "I don't want to be here" belief as the *death urge* and talk about it as stemming from the *birth death cycle.* The birth death cycle is a name for the pattern described above where unresolved feelings from birth get projected onto death, and death becomes the relief from a painful life. The death urge could be motivated by either the need to get out of the womb or the desire to get back into it.

As I have said, the desire to get back to the womb is the opposite of the need to get out of it and is equally universal and common. These two issues combined offer an explanation of how we have the need for, or dependence on relationships on one hand, and we also have the opposite issue of needing independence and freedom on the other. The solution is to work with each issue independently, thus reducing the push/pull in relationships. If the issue is about the desire to get back to the womb or away from life in a body, the affirmations are similar to those above: *"It is safe to be here," "Being here adds to my freedom,"* and *"The universe is my womb."* I would also add the most basic affirmation for the death urge, which is, *"I choose to be here."*

Even though the affirmations are similar for both sides of the issue, they will have different effects if we are aware of both sides of the push/pull issue when we use them. In the first case, where we feel the need to get out of the womb and thus relationships, we would also want to add the affirmation, *"It is safe to stay."* In the second case, where we feel compelled to get back to the womb and we might have a fear of leaving relationships as a result, we might add the affirmation, *"It is safe to leave."* Being comfortable leaving the womb, we will actually be letting go of yearning for the womb in the form of death and commit to life. The affirmation, *"It is safe to leave,"* can then actually be part of having a successful relationship because it helps free us from unwanted dependency patterns. Sometimes we cling to unsupportive "wombs" and we need to feel safe with the idea of leaving. Having the strength to leave also helps us enter relationships without dependency because the ability to leave is part of being strong and independent on our own.

In the first case, we would be using the affirmations,

"It is safe to be here,"

"I choose to be here,"

"The universe is my womb,"

and *"Relationships add to my freedom,"*

in order to get comfortable staying in relationships instead of habitually leaving. In the second case, we would be using many of those same affirmations to create the safety to leave situations that are unsupportive instead of staying in them because we are afraid to leave the womb. To be truly free, we all need to be okay staying and okay leaving, so we all benefit from the affirmations,

"It is safe to leave" and *"It is safe to stay."*

I view this as two opposing relationship skills, both of which are equally important: to be able to be yourself in a relationship, and to be able to be yourself outside of one.

The Grass is Greener

Another one of my favorite ways to add to the discussion of the Myth of the Free Spirit is to look at the notion that "the grass is greener on the other side of the hill," or the idea of "moving on to greener pastures." As previously discussed, the tendency to idealize something we don't have or fantasize that something else would be better is a core problem in relationships. On one hand, the idea of the grass being greener elsewhere highlights a basic human need to survive by improving a situation. My experience is that just as we are always improving the things in our world, like our roadways, buildings, and engineering devices, we are also compelled to improve our physical and emotional health and relationships. However, the basic human desire to build a better mousetrap results in the tendency to become dissatisfied with what we have. This obviously creates problems with consumerism and the tendency to need to buy something bigger and better than what we already have. The same impulse applies to relationships, and this perpetuates the myth of the Free Spirit and the notion that if we move away from one relationship, we will find something better. Even if this were the case, it might not be a practical risk or in our best interest because of our commitment to the interests of others.

There is tremendous value in learning to stay present in a current situation. Being here now is one way in which we honor the spiritual dimension of our lives. Allowing ourselves to be grateful for the goodness we have already received gives us more presence and power to continue to expand and manifest continued success. Being present is critical if we are to have the true power to evolve and manifest. If we are always seeking something, we are in a state of addiction where we are looking for something outside to fix our problems or make ourselves complete. When we come from a position of seeking, we are not present enough to truly receive, and we continually seek another fix. It is through being present that we can commit to someone and actually receive his or her rewards.

The drive to build a better world comes in part from feeling that we are not enough as we already are. By fantasizing that there is a better relationship out there, we are buying into our own idea that we are lacking, and we are projecting it outward by wanting to improve our situation. It is as if we are giving ourselves the message that we need to be fixed. Again, I am only applying this to people who already have a good relationship. Being in a good relationship and letting go of the idea that there is a better one is a way we can accept ourselves as good enough the way we are. This acceptance creates the presence necessary to evolve and transform. It is by accepting a good relationship as good enough that it becomes even better.

I also like to use the image or metaphor of "hovering" to further illustrate the myth of the free spirit. When we are not committed and fully in something, it is as if we are hovering above it. In the myth of the free spirit, we may be seeking freedom, but the result is that we are hovering above our lives and in a state of being removed from life and relationships. If we are not present with people or with life, we will not receive what we want from them. Trying to be a free spirit actually traps us in a hovering state. We are not fully present in our lives and are therefore not truly free to transform them.

This, like any pattern, becomes a self-fulfilling prophecy. The lack of presence leads to relationship problems, and then these problems make us want to get away; the more we try to get away, the more the problems escalate. The solution is to move into our body, life, and relationships, not away from them, and see if the increased presence or commitment transforms them. This is of course very tricky because we also have to decide if we are in a healthy relationship to which we would like to commit, or whether we are inappropriately attached to a dependant or abusive relationship, which we should develop the courage to end.

Commitment Creates Freedom

All of these points lead to what is a bigger truth about freedom, one which is actually the opposite of the myth of the free spirit: *commitment creates freedom*. The more we're involved with something, the freer we become. Real freedom comes from being present. Being present is a being state and being is freedom. By not hovering above our lives, we are present in them and more able to affect them. By feeling something fully it transforms. Note that almost all counseling or psychotherapy is about identifying and accepting feelings. This is because the more we embrace "what is," the faster it transforms naturally. This is also expressed in various spiritual practices and meditation. Zen practice is about just being with what is. When we resist things, they persist because we are not allowing them to move.

Freedom is also a virtue. Much of my work is centered on the human need to be free. In workshops, I guide people towards discovering what I call a personal purpose, which for many individuals is to be free. As I said, freedom is like love; it is an essential human need and it can always work as a guiding principle of our lives. Be clear that as I critique the negative issues around the myth of the free spirit, I am not actually talking about freedom. I am critiquing the tendency to run away from and avoid relationships or life and using the notion of freedom as a disguise for other relationship problems. Real freedom gives us the ability to commit to ourselves, our bodies, and to relationships. Conscious choice is a key to all health. Understanding each variable independently gives you an increased ability to work through un-supportive or unconscious drives and choose the relationship path that suits your whole being.

❧ PART IV ❧
FACING THE CHALLENGE

CHAPTER 34
MAINTAIN AN OPENED SYSTEM

Hopefully, this book has already helped you see what is really going on in your relationships. Perhaps it has helped you feel, accept, and begin to resolve your issues. Now, let's put the topics this book has addressed thus far into practice. Please remember that change is not a rational or linear process. Action requires shifts in feelings, so anything that helps you pay attention to the topic will serve to clear your path.

While this whole book has been a tool kit, the remaining chapters bring the process more specifically into action steps. The following sections provide additional tools for creating great, intimate, monogamous relationships. These ideas apply to creating new relationships as well as transforming existing ones.

Systems theorists in a wide variety of natural and social sciences have noted that when an organism or group is an opened system, it is more likely to grow and adapt to stress. With families and monogamous partnerships, this means that the more opened the relationship is to the world outside of it, the better. Here the word opened does not mean sexually opened or non-monogamous; it means opened to outside influence. Even counseling is an act of opening a relationship to outside input. The system becomes more stable as a result.

When a system is closed, it is more likely to have entropy. Entropy is a term that describes how a system left on its own is more likely to stop progressing and literally stop moving. Most of the dictionary definitions of entropy are applicable here, but two key definitions are, "A hypothetical tendency for all matter and energy in the universe to evolve toward a state of inert uniformity;" and "inevitable and steady deterioration of a system or society." When a system is isolated, it is more likely to stop progressing or moving, thus becoming inert and uniform because it has less variables of interaction. With fewer variables interacting, the ones that remain will become more and more the same (inert and uniform) because each time they interact, they become closer to each other. They eventually exhaust themselves because they are not stimulating each other. This could explain part of any relationship issue, such as how communication can deteriorate. One person has a hurt, they shut down, don't communicate, and withdraw, and then the other does something similar. Pretty soon, they are feeding each other's dysfunction by recycling it.

Seeing the value of maintaining an opened system can be further understood by realizing how a relationship that is a closed system is unhealthy. An extreme example of a closed system is how abusers tend to try to isolate their partners from outside influence by restricting friendships or outside interests. A phenomenon similar to how abusers isolate their victims often occurs when two people fall in love and prefer being alone with their partner because it is so nice to have a relationship. The result may be similar to how things were when they were single. When someone is single and wants a partnership, their isolation, aloneness, or low self-esteem issues make them a closed system. Then when they meet a partner, they rush to make the relationship a system that will save them from their aloneness. What happens instead is they close their partnership off to the outside world as a means of remaining safe. They may have exchanged one form of isolation for another. What used to be "me against the world" becomes "us against the world."

A healthier context is to view our lives as bigger than just our relationship. Our life is about our own identity and healing, our career, family, health, spirituality, and more. By viewing our primary relationship as one large part of a whole, we put our relationship into a system that is larger than itself. Our identity as an individual is the primary aspect of our lives and is actually the only constant in our lives. Our lives are part of a system that is always changing. By standing on our own with strength, we don't try to hold on to or posses relationships, which is one step toward giving relationships room to breathe and grow. No matter how solid a relationship is, it is always possible that some set of variables could occur that would lead to it changing or ending. Realizing this keeps us humble and reminds us to continue to process our issues. To say that we will never change the form of our relationship is too absolute and creates a closed system. It can also increase the chance of being blind-sided by an attraction and acting more unconsciously as a result.

As long as we are also embracing our commitment and working to resolve the ways in which we may want to avoid or escape from intimacy, it can be helpful to realize that we do not know for sure if a relationship will last forever. To say that we will never divorce gives both partners too much permission to slack off and neglect the relationship. It may even give our partner permission to mistreat us. To be married "in the moment" is valuable because it forces us to be committed to the quality of the relationship and to be committed to ourselves first. Realizing that it is possible that our relationship could change and no longer be healthy is a key to negotiating from strength. It forces both parties to react and respond to each other in the moment and treat each other as human beings and not as possessions. To say that we will *never* separate actually closes the system of a relationship. Instead, I actually recommend that we *never say never.*

It is valuable to view our relationship as part of a larger community and to allow that community to be part of our relationship. This simply means that we have and maintain outside friendships. Addressing privacy issues is key here because what I am suggesting is that if we don't have two or three outside friends, and probably a therapist, who know us well, then we are probably in too closed of a system. The act of confiding in a friend is deeply metaphysical. It does all the things that abusers instinctually know when they try to isolate their victims. It helps an individual see and feel what they want, need and deserve. It helps people understand what is normal, and if their situation is abnormal, it helps them confront it. It also helps them grow and move forward. Having a friend who knows your direction helps you stay conscious and committed to it yourself. Our friends, teachers, and counselors act as "poles" in our lives, and they create added strength and stability.

Isolation is an inherent problem with nuclear families and our loss of tribal culture. Even the fact that most of us rent or own separate housing cubicles makes it harder for us to have an opened system. Our personal and work schedules are virtually compartmentalized. Most of us work way more than primitive cultures did in the past, leaving less time and energy to develop personal relationships or spirituality. To avoid being abused by power inequalities at work, we make sure not to get too close to the people there. Additionally, we not only have less personal time but we also live in a relatively isolated fashion. Just the notion that we have separate business and personal lives illustrates my point. We have lost rich potential by separating family, work, and community. Capitalism has increased our isolation by taking our workday out of our homes and family business.

Systems theory suggests that what is more natural and needed is to have life and relationships to be one broad system. If our days were filled with continual contact with people of importance, our life would have more support and meaning. Ideally, our life would be like a tapestry, where people, places, and things are all interwoven and connected. We all need to work to make our personal and business lives more meaningful and connected to our identities as people.

CHAPTER 35
THE ROLE OF SPIRITUAL AND SERVICE COMMUNITIES

It is also valuable to open up our system by participating in spiritual and service communities. I define spiritual community as any group of friends who acknowledge that part of their bond is to support each other's spiritual growth. This could be a church, a support or therapy group, a yoga studio, or it could be something less overtly spiritual, such as a chess, car, or quilting club. A service community is a group that dedicates itself to giving service to others or the environment, such as a charity or volunteer tree-planting program.

It has often been said that if you want to handle a problem, take on a bigger one. Spirituality and service are different ideals, but they both help us expand beyond our own personal needs. They help us view our relationships as larger than ourselves, and they draw us out and beyond our own lives. This makes our problems appear smaller and easier to resolve.

The more accepting the community is, the better. Having a spiritual community that can feel and know our relationship strengths and weaknesses and love us without judgment really opens our system. It is hard to allow all aspects of ourselves to grow and move freely without taboos. It helps us if our community has minimal dogma that makes us feel that we should have a certain kind of partnership or be a certain kind of person. This does not mean that churches with strong ideals and rules are bad communities; it just means that the stronger the set of rules, the more closed the system.

A Service community or the act of increasing our service in the world does the same thing. By helping others, we transcend our own issues because ours become smaller in our mind. As a result, we work through them more easily. By working to solve bigger problems that are outside of our own self-interest, we gain a better perspective from which to view our own challenges. As suggested earlier, sometimes the best way to handle a problem is to take on a bigger one; however, it is important not to use service as a way to avoid our own issues. I have heard of many people who were revered in the world but not liked at home. It is also just simply annoying and ineffective if someone is giving to others but is not in touch with themselves. While serving others could be an act of avoiding our own issues, if it is combined with a psycho-spiritual approach of facing our own issues, it serves to accelerate our own personal growth. If we work on our own lives while helping others, it has a dynamic positive effect on everyone involved.

On some level, all careers (except crime) are service careers. Virtually all of us are engaged in providing goods or services to the world. Some careers provide more direct contact with the customer than others and thus may result in a more direct feeling that we have served or made a difference, but ultimately we are all involved in delivering a good or service. We might be a teacher who is educating future generations, a construction worker who is creating housing or roads, a hot dog vendor providing convenient fast food, or a homemaker who is serving their children and thus society. If we remember that our work is service, we can reap more rewards from it.

Additionally, it is valuable to serve beyond our work life or our personal need for the money we generate there. The act of participating in a service organization or project that is outside of our own day-to-day interest is more unconditional and thus has a deeper impact. I feel that I would be a hypocrite if I lived my upwardly mobile lifestyle and did not dedicate time and money to service. No matter how challenged I have felt financially, I benefit by remembering that I have basic abundance: I have a car, I regularly eat in restaurants, and I spend money for entertainment. By giving something beyond my own expenses, I remember my own abundance.

CHAPTER 36
TELLING THE TRUTH

Telling the truth, first to ourselves and then ideally to others, is a simple yet profound relationship aide. It can be thought of as an essential ground rule for successful relationships, but it is also a profound metaphysical principle. By expressing a truth, it has the opportunity to transform. By bringing it out into the open, our feelings and issues associated with it receive the attention and "light" they need to move freely. If we hold a feeling or issue in secret, it stays trapped within us. It becomes closeted, because the same energy we spend making sure not to expose it results in our holding it tightly. Telling the truth exposes our feelings and issues to the "light," and in the open, we see them and admit them more fully. This helps us deal with them and resolve them.

By telling the truth, I don't just mean answering questions truthfully. Telling the truth means voluntarily disclosing relevant information. If someone were having an affair, telling the truth wouldn't mean being prepared to answer truthfully while hoping and praying that the question never comes. Telling the truth would mean disclosing the fact because it is relevant, and their partner would want to know.

Not disclosing the truth could be seen as lying. It is valuable to get comfortable with the word lie. Whether we hold back by omitting important information about ourselves, or by directly speaking things that are not true, the word lie addresses the issues involved. We lie when we don't speak up about what we need in an intimate relationship. We lie when we censor our dreams, and we lie when we omit information we fear will make others upset. Having secrets is like having a black hole that drains the energy from our relationships. From this view, any withheld information is a lie. The term "withhold" is another valuable way to describe this issue.

Everyone is "psychic." We subconsciously know what is going on and if there is something being held back. While we may not consciously feel an upset about it, the information that is held back creates a barrier to full intimacy. Thinking of it this way can help us take the risk of speaking up. The truth is felt on some level, and speaking up will give it light. The relationship will have the opportunity to move toward growth and healing. If we express a truth and the relationship dissolves, it helps us to realize that the relationship was probably irrevocably damaged from the withheld information in the first place.

Withholds, secrets, and lies also act within our psyche in much the same way disowned selves do. The energy we spend avoiding the issues and keeping them suppressed results in them building strength. By disclosing the truths and feelings, we "lighten up" about them, and they can more easily move and release. These same principles apply to our personal growth, therapy, and friendships. We all need to take the lead on being the one to share ourselves in order for intimacy to deepen. If intimacy means *in-to-me–*

see, then opening ourselves to the people with whom we choose to be intimate is essential and not something anyone else can do for us. We need to learn to speak up.

It is important to resolve the difficulties we have expressing the truth as a result of family and social conditioning. We have been trained to fear our feelings and to hide them because we are afraid that expressing them will upset others. We tend to hold back and try to say what will please others instead. Withholding our feelings is a key relationship problem on its own, but it also fosters other relationship issues by keeping them hidden. Whatever the truth, the process of learning to speak up about it is very healing, and it also helps resolve the issue by giving light to other specific issues.

This does not mean I am entirely opposed to lying. I feel it is human nature to lie when we feel threatened. If a child steals candy and lies about it, I see two problems: the theft and the lie. With regard to the lie, who is responsible for lying? The child may have needed to lie to avoid the parent's punitive nature.

There are times when lying to protect ourselves is appropriate. If we feel we are in this situation, the next key is to determine whether the threat is real or if we are afraid to tell the truth because of old conditioning. Ultimately, we have to decide if we are in a situation where we want intimacy and it is safe to pursue it by disclosing and making amends for the lie, or if we are in a shame-based environment where the truth will be held against us. In blunt terms, I would never fault someone for lying to a tyrant. I would question the wisdom of being intimately involved with one. It is actually possible that it is important to lie to minimize the damage that leaving a tyrant could bring us. As it is possible that having an affair is one way someone could gain the strength to leave a tyrant, it might also be practical to withhold from them knowledge of the affair.

In most cases, it is safer and more important to tell the truth than we realize. A key to telling the truth is to first become more comfortable with it within us. Being afraid of certain feelings or emotions results in a tendency to hide our own truths from ourselves. The fear of feeling is linked to the fear of others' reactions to our feelings. Basically, most of us have family and societal issues where upsetting feelings are taboo and the expression of them is doubly taboo.

The fear of expressing the truth has been widely discussed within dysfunctional family, codependency, and recovery literature. Here, I would like to outline one key piece of the puzzle. The vast majority of us were parented in a way that encouraged us to suppress our feelings and identity in order to do what our parents wanted. If our parents had validated our truths, we would feel more secure expressing ourselves. The peak of the issue comes from not allowing children who are two to five years of age to say no or to express negativity or disagreement. If we embrace a child's identity and truths (even if they make us uncomfortable), they will develop as strong individuals who are less dependant on other people's opinions. This is the central component of codependency issues.

Children need to have their truth validated as often as possible. When we do, we teach them that it is okay to have an independent identity. This identity is what people need to speak up and tell the truth to friends, partners, and bosses. This identity is, by the way, what a child or adult needs to be able to say no to a potential abuser.

This does not mean that we do not say no to a child. If we are clear with the limits and boundaries we set, our kids will be less likely to test us with emotional outbursts or tantrums. Tantrums are likely to be frequent if they help the child get what they want. If a parent gives in to tantrums, they become the child's way of trying to get power or get their way. Some tantrums are normal because they are one way for a child to release pent up feelings, which build up because they are less able to articulate them.

There is an important balance between allowing kids a strong sense of self and setting appropriate limits. If we keep the boundaries we set with kids to the important issues and leave room for them to make choices on their own or disagree with us, it helps them develop a healthy identity. There are key limits that we should never negotiate with children. I view them as safety and respect of self, others, and property. Health and nutrition are also rarely negotiable. By *picking our battles* and focusing on the important issues, we teach our kids that others are important, too, and we give them room to be and develop themselves.

My intent here is to give one picture of why we might fear expressing the truth—our parents probably invalidated us constantly, in large and small ways. Our parents' love may have seemed conditional and based on whether or not we behaved according to their expectations. One way to summarize the result of this is that we fear that by saying no we will lose love. The affirmations *"I have the right to say no without losing love"* and *"I can express my feelings without losing love"* have always been important ones.

Many of us had scary experiences as children, where our parents' (or others') anger scared us, thus furthering the taboos against expressing anger. In order to resolve many of the issues and these taboos, I recommend therapies where we learn to allow and express strong emotions. There are many safe ways that therapists help people contact and express old anger in therapy. I do not recommend that this anger be directed toward anyone in person; for example, I do not allow couples to yell at each other. When I do this work, I do it individually and in private with the client yelling at a chair or pillow that represents the person with whom they are angry. Emotive therapies offer value in two big ways: first, they help us deal with our issues; and second, they help us resolve the taboos on feeling emotions in general. Most of us will benefit from the affirmation, *"My anger is safe and innocent."*

Once we are on the path of learning to tell the truth, it becomes important to learn to express ourselves *gently and responsibly.* Telling the truth does not give license to be cold, critical, or verbally abusive. I have never met anyone who "can take it as well as they can dish it out." We are all sensitive beings, and it is simply destructive and impractical if we express ourselves in a way that is hurtful. Given our sensitive natures, we are likely to cause some hurt feelings even if we express ourselves gently and responsibly. This is a challenging issue where we need to address the truth of our feelings while maintaining sensitivity.

Gentle communication can be difficult to achieve because it is not simply a soft voice or stature that make the communications gentle. Often we try to be gentle but have aggressive or angry selves that are still present or dominant. Unresolved anger will usually be felt by others or will tend to leak out. To be truly gentle, we need to do the deeper inner work to shift the feelings and selves involved so that our whole being becomes gentle with the relationship or communication. Virtually everyone will make errors with their voice and the hidden or unconscious energies within it. This is an area where we need to be patient with ourselves and understand that it is normal to make errors. If our partner reacts negatively, it may be a sign that we were in a voice, and we need to continue to look closer at the energy we are putting out.

We also need to take *responsibility* for our reactions to what people express to us. Responsibility is a second key to healthy truth telling. When we say, "We need to take responsibility for our feelings," we are saying that it is important to remember that our feelings and reactions are based on our own issues and perceptions and not necessarily on any objective reality.

The dictionary definition of responsibility is "a source or cause." This is the case with our feelings; we are the source or cause of them. Our reactions are always based on our perspective, and our perspective is unique to us. I view relationships as two cultures relating. Our relationship conflicts are based on how two people's unique histories and inner cultures are intersecting or colliding. In cultural anthropology, the term ethnocentrism is used to describe our difficulty in accepting another culture's practices, and more specifically refers to the belief that our own culture is superior to others. When we have difficulty taking responsibility for our feelings or reactions to another, we are making a similar error of arrogance.

Repeating a popular definition of culture is also helpful here. Culture is often defined as rules and norms that govern appropriate behavior. We all have inner rules and norms (many of which are unconscious), which shape our preferences. This is an aspect of our identity, and we need to take responsibility for the way it affects how we view others and relate to them. Our way is not necessarily the right way; it is just our primary way. It is as deeply embedded into our consciousness as any cultural practice is embedded in a culture, or any belief is embedded in a religion. This applies to all issues, big and small. Our feelings or opinions are based on our own history, culture, or preferences.

In the framework of psychological or spiritual work, it is most likely unresolved family or birth issues that affect our responses to people. If we harshly judge someone who is having an affair, it is probably because it triggers our old issues with affairs or our fear of abandonment. If we dislike someone's personality, it is because their personality is triggering something that is unresolved from a prior relationship or from within ourselves. For example, if we judge someone who is talkative, it might be because they trigger an unresolved relationship issue we have with someone who was talkative, or because they are different from our own inner rule that it is best to be quiet. If we think someone doesn't like us, we need to take responsibility that this might be our perception based on our low self-esteem issues.

You may feel that you know this and understand how to take responsibility in your relationships, but I want to emphasize that it requires ongoing focus. We all have areas where we have blind spots. Our relationship upsets exist because we have unresolved issues that are being expressed in the way we interact both physically and metaphysically. Whenever we have a "charge" with a person or situation, it is because we have something we need to look at or for which we must take responsibility. Even people who are experienced with relationship, or metaphysical workings, forget to take responsibility for their feelings or perceptions. This can be exacerbated by their using the tools and awareness they have to disguise their own reactions and/or become skilled at analyzing the other person's issues or behavior. Often people learn to do this while maintaining a calm or authoritative front to hide their own issues.

This does not mean we should withhold or avoid our reactions. If we don't deal with our reactions to each other, then we are missing the richness and the growth that our relationships are offering. We need to acknowledge our reactions to each other and take responsibility for what is reactive within us. We also need to address our feelings and find appropriate ways to tell the truth to each other. This is so complex that we are sure to make mistakes, but this is part of the process, and we can clean them up as we go.

Another area of interest in learning to tell the truth is to "put our worst foot forward." This is about becoming able to let ourselves be seen "warts and all." Putting our worst foot forward means beginning a relationship without pretense. If we harbor something that we fear will create rejection, it is best to get it out and over with early. If someone rejects us for it, it reveals that there is not much substance in the relationship. By risking rejection, we break our people-pleasing and codependency tendencies. This does not mean that we share what is wrong with us as a primary way of connecting and creating sympathy, or use our issues or pain to put ourselves in a victim role with another. Putting our worst foot forward means not hiding. This notion is valuable for people who have a past where they tried to look good and maintain appearances. Honesty creates intimacy, and it is never too early to be honest. If we come from a relaxed or playful place with this, it results in an innocent way to deepen intimacy. You can make it an exercise or game, where you disclose the reasons the other might not want to have a relationship with you early in the dating process.

CHAPTER 37
LIVING FOR TWO OR MORE:
COMMITMENT, CONSCIENCE, INTEGRITY, AND LOYALTY

Love is an all-encompassing quality that is most noticed in the absence of negative thought or patterns. Our ability to love exists within and beyond our complex issues. Our love for our partner can be enough to transcend any problem, such as a sexual attraction to another. Even if more work is required, love is a variable that always works and assists our process. While monogamy is not as simple as love, commitment, conscience, integrity, and loyalty, focusing on these qualities helps us to use our spiritual selves to manifest monogamy and the relationships we want.

To commit to another is to love and care for them and for what they need. Being able to consider the needs of the people we love is a very advanced relationship skill. In child development, it is sometimes said that a child can't fully consider another persons needs until age sixteen. The issue is complicated for adults, too, given that we're all still growing in the various ways in which we care for ourselves and for others.

I have said much about the problems associated with caretaking and being overly focused on what others need, or not being able to ask for what we need. While resolving these issues is central to creating successful relationships, there are also important issues that can appear to be the opposite. These involve our inability to include what the other person needs into what we need. As we become better at feeling we deserve what we want, we also need to become better at being aware of what other people want. In the end, being able to feel our own needs and their importance while simultaneously acknowledging the importance and validity of our partner's or loved one's needs results in the highest level of intimacy and the most conscious relationship choices. It takes a strong identity and character to be able to honor what another person needs. When our identity or self-esteem is low, we are more likely to be narcissistic and spend energy trying to assert our importance. As we get stronger, we actually become better equipped to include other people in our needs and plans.

It requires maturity to consider what others need as part of what we need. Think of the times that a partner has been inconsiderate of your needs. Remembering how it feels to be on the receiving end of the lack of consideration will remind you of the importance of love and kindness. For example, have you ever been dumped by someone in a cold or irresponsible manner? It is important to act conscientiously and with awareness as to how our actions are going to affect others. We might need to leave a relationship, but feeling compassion will help us act in a clearer and more humane way.

To resolve conflicts within a partnership, we need to consider our partner's needs. This also means that we may choose to stay in a partnership because we don't want to hurt our partner or our children. It is a valid choice to stay in a relationship that has difficulties, especially if that choice is a conscious one. This could simply feel like wanting to stay because the relationship is more okay than it is bad, and we would prefer to work on the difficulties rather than separate. What is tricky about this route is that we might also be acting on old caretaking or codependency rules by staying in a bad situation. Many people are actually in abusive marriages where all parties, including the children, would be better served by separating than by continuing.

If we consider staying in a relationship where we are unhappy, it is important to evaluate whether our motives are based on the fear of being alone, or the old rules of caretaking, people pleasing, or doing what others want. In any case, conscious choice can only be made after we understand both sides of the issue. One side is maintaining a relationship because of love and the other is maintaining it out of fear. This is a huge question, which can only be answered by each individual. An additional question that helps frame the issue is, are we being too selfish or not selfish enough? Most people need to be more selfish, and once we are selfish in a healthy sense, we have greater ability to incorporate others' needs. If we choose to leave a relationship, it is important not to come from a place of rebellion but instead from a place of greater self-care.

This topic is more simply applied to maintaining monogamy within a relationship we intend to keep. It hurts most people quite deeply if their partner has sexual contact with another. Remembering this and being able to put ourselves in their shoes is a basic way to stay strong and avoid affairs. If we can simultaneously feel both our desire to have an affair and our desire not to hurt our partner or children, we can put our sexual desire in a bigger context and more easily choose not to act on it. In this way, qualities like commitment, loyalty, integrity, and conscience enable us to make more aware choices that are based on our heart's greater desires. Sometimes these words imply that we are behaving in a way that is purely designed to do what other people need, but it is important to connect with how the other person's needs and our own are similar. This helps us do what we really need and not act on one aspect of ourselves, such as sexual desire.

This is one simple reason I never had an affair in my sixteen-year marriage. I didn't want to have lies, and I didn't want to cause my wife pain. No amount of shortcomings within our partnership would have made me feel she deserved that. If you have a partnership, my hope for you is that your partnership succeeds in creating ever-increasing nourishment and passion for both of you. Remembering these ideas of conscience and loyalty will help you commit to creating positive energy in your relationship. Increased commitment, conscience, integrity, and loyalty can help motivate you to use attractions to identify and incorporate what you need into your existing relationship.

It is important to incorporate these values beyond the arena of having affairs. They also apply to the partner with less sexual desire being committed to working on their issues and creating a good sexual relationship. The partner with less sexual desire is acting with integrity when they actively work on their issues and seek more sexual connection in the partnership. The same notions should be applied to non-sexual issues like being a committed and loyal partner with shared parenting, homemaking, and financial responsibility. It is an act of conscience, loyalty, and integrity when we maintain our agreements or equality in all areas.

Many couples do not talk about their expectations within their partnership but instead assume that their commitment or relationship will take a certain form. I am not suggesting that if you didn't negotiate something up front then you have no right to expect it; however, other marriage issues of shared responsibility are integrity issues, and we too often want our loyalty to be simple and restricted to the areas of monogamy or money. For example, in a one income heterosexual partnership, where the man earns the income, he might have assumed that his primary responsibility was to earn money and maintain a monogamous commitment, while the woman might have assumed that he would also help raise the children. In this case, the couple would then need to consciously discuss the issue and decide on fair expectations.

These kinds of subtleties are loyalty and integrity issues, which if not handled fairly, are in fact betrayals that could be equal to having an affair. Verbal or physical abuse is another kind of betrayal that is equal to having an affair. All deceptions are painful. Lying about money, speaking harshly to your partner, or breaking childrearing agreements also damage the trust within your relationship. When we enter into a partnership, it is fair to assume that we will be treated kindly. Having an affair is by no means the only way in which we betray our commitment to our partner.

CHAPTER 38
DEVOTION VS. LOYALTY: GETTING BEYOND BETRAYAL

I was at a small gathering where the topic of male sexuality came up, and a female acquaintance of mine, who was implying that monogamy was not natural for men, said, "I have come to accept that all men have a little dog in them." To this I responded, "You mean they are forever loyal and devoted." While I wouldn't have written this book if I didn't understand that men sometimes lack a conscience in the sexual arenas of their lives, I also feel that men are hardworking and loyal. Just as men sometimes complain about feeling like "beasts of burden," they are also dogged and will fight fiercely for the people they love.

Overall, I prefer the notion of devotion to loyalty because it affirms more positive feelings than loyalty does. Devotion describes our need to give love, and loyalty infers that we are doing what someone else wants. The dictionary definition that is most important to me is that devotion is "ardent, often selfless affection and dedication." To me, the term devotion clearly implies that we have the need to love and commit—it is a human need to place our love and affections with another. While loyalty is a good thing, I feel it might trigger obligation, possession, or rebellion. Devotion

251

holds more unconditional love than loyalty does. Just as we all need to be loved, and feel that we belong in the world, we all also need *to* love and to commit and devote ourselves to others. Just as we actively seek love, it is also natural to help others feel loved.

Any confusion we might have about this is primarily based on fear; meaning that our feelings of devotion are often clouded by our fears around abandonment, losing our freedom, or of becoming obligated. We are afraid to give deeply because we are afraid of rejection or loss; or we are afraid of losing ourselves. I maintain that a strong individual with a strong identity, who is free of the myth of being a free spirit, is naturally free to love deeply and that this is our natural state.

For many people, the fear of devotion seems to be more central because of the fears of abandonment, loss of freedom, and suffocation. Perhaps more so for men than women because of the kinds of biological and anthropological issues I cited in part III. Devotion needs more emphasis in our lives, and understanding it will help balance any lifestyle, increase intimacy, and of course help maintain monogamy in the midst of our other problems and desires.

Rethinking the intensity with which we use the word betrayal is also helpful. When someone is not monogamous, especially if they lie about it, it is a betrayal. But, when we define the issue as betrayal, we highlight their accountability to us instead of treating them as a free and sovereign individual with the right to change or make new choices. It is helpful to see that the need to move away from a relationship is not actually a betrayal. If anything, it is lying that makes for betrayal. The ultimate betrayal is when we betray our own inner voice, values, integrity, rules, commitment, or conscience. When someone has an affair, the betrayal is upsetting, but it is also upsetting that they have betrayed their own desire for a sacred, monogamous relationship.

I have found that the most basic form my need for devotion takes is to give enthusiastically and unconditionally to my partner. It also goes beyond that to include giving to children, friends, parents, community, organizations, and the environment. Devotion can accentuate dependency issues, and I have created an important balance in my life by remembering to express my devotional side trans-personally in spiritual and service practices. These have helped me balance my loving nature so that my need to love did not overly weigh down my relationships.

CHAPTER 39
LETTING GO OF AN APOLOGETIC NATURE

Apology is very important and often overlooked. Apologizing when appropriate helps heal upsets. It is called for when we have made errors and seek to make amends. In these situations, apology is the opposite of defensiveness or justification. Often, when we have legitimately angered another, all they really need is to be listened to and have their feelings validated. Apologizing is part of this.

Other times, apology can be a shame-based issue, where we are apologizing unnecessarily as if we are apologizing for being alive. Sometimes we apologize for the details about who we are, when what would be more purposeful is for us to have self-esteem and feel innocent about our uniqueness. For example, there is no need to apologize for having sexual desire or more sexual desire than our partner. If our desire has led to groping our partner and making them uncomfortable, then we can apologize for that, but the essence of our sexuality needs no apology. There is no need to apologize unnecessarily; instead, we should feel innocent and accepting of ourselves. This is particularly important if we have adopted an apologetic nature and tend to apologize for things that we shouldn't.

We can feel innocent about our desire without making another person wrong for their desire (or lack of it) or forcing them to comply.

The value of feeling innocent is that it will help us approach our desire from strength and worthiness, which will enable us to manifest what we truly want. If we feel guilty for having desire, it will negatively affect how we ask for what we need. Guilt will add to the problem of not asking for what we need and can result in aggressive, defensive, or coercive behavior. If we feel innocent, we won't feel the need to hide our desire or fight to get what we want. Innocence gives us the ability to ask for what we want cleanly so our partner will be able to respond to us without adding his or her own guilt, shame, or defensiveness to the issue.

CHAPTER 40
BEING SENSITIVE ABOUT SEXUAL ABUSE AND SEXUAL OBJECTIFICATION

While I am clearly asserting the importance of feeling innocent about our sexual desire for our partner, it is very important that we be sensitive as to how our desire might trigger their issues. Perhaps the most important example is if someone has unresolved sexual abuse issues. They will be more likely to resist sexual advances. Our sexual advances will likely be felt as our wanting something from them instead of our wanting to give something to them.

The therapy community has devoted much attention to this, and it is also an important topic for this book. That said, it is also important to note that past sexual abuse does not always result in sexual difficulties or in people having low sexual desire. But, if our partner feels triggered by our advances, whether a source of the upset is past abuse or not, it is important to be sensitive and work together to develop ways not to become polarized with them feeling prodded or poked by our desire.

Another key issue that connects sexual abuse issues to everyone is the notion of sexual objectification. The sexual objectification of women is a paramount problem for us to work through and solve if we are going to have healthy relationships. Men are sexually objectified, too, but less so than women, and men's sexual objectification also gives them more benefits. While men are treated as objects, the patriarchal nature of society also places them in the superior or more powerful position. Objectification is a dual edge sword for men, where as for women, the effects are more negative. Some women have learned to gain power by manipulating men with their sexuality, but I would still describe women's status overall as being beneath men. Treating women like sex objects is part of this.

Being treated like an object, thing, or commodity is demeaning. It makes us feel uncared for. While having sexual desire for our partner is probably very different from our treating them like an object, it can trigger the greater belief that sex is all we are good for, or that old belief that "men only want one thing." Talking about how advertising, movies, magazines, and literature portray men and women is an easy way to begin to get in touch with this. Many of these give both men and women the message that they must look or perform a certain way to measure up. Women are told that what is most important is their looks and sexuality, and men are told that what is most important is their power, financial status, and sexuality. It is fair to say that the sexual nature of this issue has been worse for women.

Most of the women we know grew up with constant images that implied it was their beauty and sexual value that defined them and made them worthy of love. This has led to resentments that are triggered if women feel that our primary interest in them is for sex. People need to feel that all of them is loved and accepted. When we focus on one aspect of someone's value, such as physical beauty, more than others, it will trigger resistance and rebellion. It is natural to resist conditional love.

It is valuable to connect this point to the idea that on average women are more spiritual and emotionally developed than men, and women's sexuality is more connected to their heart than men's sexuality. Women are more likely to want love to be expressed and demonstrated in a variety of nonsexual ways in order to feel sexual. Women are more likely to need a more spiritual and emotional basis for sex, and approaching a woman in a purely sexual way is more likely to make her feel objectified. Men also have emotional and spiritual needs, and they need sex to incorporate those needs, but men are on average more likely to enjoy being approached directly for sex than women are. Perhaps the key to a woman's heart lies in the kitchen, where a man's lies in the bedroom.

If you sexually desire a woman, it is valuable to realize that when you tell her she is beautiful, she might be hearing more than a compliment. She might be hearing that you require her to be beautiful, or that you "want just one thing." If this becomes the case, she might feel objectified, and her interest is more likely to be lost. If she feels loved for her entire being and not just her physical body, she will be more likely to remain connected to her own sexual desires.

I recommend that men make sure to complement women on more than just their physical beauty or clothing. As a relationship develops, it is helpful to learn about how a woman feels about being told she is beautiful. While most women need to be told they look good and are beautiful, some are also triggered by it and need more focus on their intellectual, spiritual, and emotional strengths. Keep in mind that it is almost always safe to acknowledge someone for his or her mental or spiritual qualities. It is in the areas of sex and money that problems are more likely to occur.

If you have desire for a man, it would be a good idea to have a similar sensitivity and try to discover what kind of acknowledgement works best for him. If a man (or woman) is wealthy, for example, they might have a concern that people only care about them because of the money they have. If this were the case, you would want to avoid focusing too much on money and seek to make it clear that it was his company, intellect, and body that you most desired. This is tricky though, because if he were paying for dinner or a vacation, some thanks would be appropriate. This brings us back to creating a similar balance with women. On one hand, a woman might not want her beauty objectified, but on the other hand, she might want to hear that you feel she is beautiful.

Relationships are complex, and there are sometimes conflicting "hoops" through which to jump. It can be as if there are two different hoops that only partly overlap, and you have to hit the small opening where both hoops agree. Once again, perfectionism is not necessary—if you work with these variables as best you can, you will be well on your way towards creating real intimacy.

I have said that the sexual objectification of women has been greater than that of men; however, the objectification of men as financial or power brokers has been greater than that of women. Men tend to feel like beasts of burden, and their ability to create money is what makes them worthy. In this way, it is easy for a man to feel objectified as a financial commodity. The cultural objectification of men's sexuality is also increasing. I watch a lot of movies with my sons, and there is no question that they are getting the message from the entertainment industry that if they are not handsome, prosperous, and good lovers, they will be dumped. If you don't measure up, don't even bother to have desire; don't even try to connect with the girl unless you look, act, and have a car like (insert sexy rich character/actor's name here). It is painful to feel like we are an object or *thing*. To feel truly desired, we need to feel that our *being* is wanted. We need to feel desired for our mind, body, and soul. Paying equal attention to all the ways we love each other will help us let in the love.

Paying attention to our partner in all the ways we love them will reduce the power struggles that might occur if they feel objectified. Good communication and listening results in them feeling loved and respected for their mind and emotions. Helping with chores or serving our partner shows love and respect for his or her whole being, body and soul. Sharing money and seeking to maximize earnings and minimize spending shows respect on all levels, too. Non-sexual touch demonstrates love beyond sex, and it shows unconditional caring for what our partner feels. Non-sexual touch helps people feel loved because the exchange is one way from giver to receiver. The receiver is more likely to feel unconditionally loved because it is quite clear that the giver is not receiving as much. When we share housework or parenting responsibilities, we show that we know these are important, and it communicates to our partner that we value their housework and parenthood.

Acknowledgement in the form of words that express thanks to our partner for what they do for us is important, but actions demonstrate our love and appreciation more deeply than words.

It is helpful if we remember that our physical attractions are largely based on our emotional and spiritual connections. This becomes more and more the case as we evolve emotionally, sexually, and spiritually. The more developed we are as emotional and spiritual beings, and the more our sexuality is connected to our emotions and spirituality, the more our physical desire will be a complete expression of our emotional and spiritual connection. If we think of what makes us really attracted to someone, it is easy to see that it is more than just physical. While we might be attracted to some set of standardized physical ideals, most people are far more drawn to the people with whom they also share an emotional or spiritual connection. Likewise, when we have a strong connection with someone, we find them beautiful regardless of how their beauty fits into standardized ideals. So, it helps if we remember that when someone wants us physically, it is not just physical; they're desiring our entire being. Desiring our body is a great way for them to express it.

CHAPTER 41
BEING SENSITIVE WITHOUT LOSING YOUR MASCULINITY

Years ago, I coined an acronym that has either gotten around or been thought of independently, which is the Sensitive New Age Guy, or SNAG. It is great to be a Sensitive New Age Guy, but it is hard to do without losing your masculinity.

Relationships work best when we learn to be sensitive to the needs of the other, while still holding ourselves as important. This would include feeling good about our own uniqueness, which may include our masculinity. Men may be naturally more direct, less verbal, and less emotional than women are. Relationships work best if men are sensitive and are themselves. Masculinity does not inherently make men insensitive, but it is a strong and powerful quality that can be lost if men reject it in favor of being sensitive. Sensitivity and masculinity are not opposites, but it can be particularly challenging for men to be sensitive and also embody their own individuality, which might be more masculine than their partner's.

On one hand, most emotionally and spiritually developed women want sensitive partners, and on the other hand, they want their partners to be themselves. If heterosexual women wanted men to be women, they probably wouldn't be heterosexual. Well-developed men who have a strong sensitive side are often referred to as having a well-developed feminine (or feeling side). This is a good thing because it enables a man to navigate the kinds of ideas expressed in this book. It is great if men are feminists with strong inner matriarchies. But if a man's masculine side is suppressed or is not present, something will be felt as lacking. It would be hard to feel his whole being. If his masculine side is suppressed, his sensitive side would also have less meaning, since it would have nothing to help ground it to other aspects of his authentic nature.

In psycho-spiritual teachings, the terms masculine and feminine are often used to describe tendencies that are separate from sex or gender. Men have feminine energy just as women have masculine energy. When we use these terms independently of gender, we describe masculine energy as independent and feminine energy as relationship oriented. Masculine energy is powerful, authoritative, rational, and solitary. Feminine energy is receptive, supportive, feeling, and intimate. Another common way to reference masculine and feminine energy is using the Chinese terms of yin to describe the feminine and yang to describe the masculine component. The yin/yang symbol

refers to how the two combine to make up a whole and shows how the two energies feed each other. It helps to take the issue out the area of sex and gender and reminds us that we need both energies to be whole.

Ultimately, we are better served by not labeling something as masculine or feminine. It is better to be more specific and cite the human qualities underneath the terms. When we attribute a quality to be either masculine or feminine, we imply that one gender will always have more of that quality than the other. While there may be real differences between men and women, when we let go of the labels, it creates more openings for us to grow in both our masculine and feminine nature. Instead of using labels, we could make reference to how our independence needs or our intimacy needs are affecting our relationship.

Problems can arise in relationships if men suppress their masculinity in their desire to be sensitive. While there is not any one right way to have or begin a relationship, many therapy clients still seem to be tied to older cultural norms where the man is expected to initiate the first significant contacts. In heterosexual dating, part of us still expects a man to ask the woman out on a date and pay for it. If the feminist side of our culture has consciously or unconsciously told the man not to be a predator or a "horny dog," then he may sit back and be too afraid to initiate contact.

If women continue with the older norms, where they are expected to be more passive, then nobody initiates relationships. Everyone should initiate contact if they want it. But given that we are currently operating with conflicting rules on the subject, we need to relax and not shame men for being aggressive while also encouraging women to pursue men when they want.

It is also correct to hypothesize that men do essentially carry some biological or spiritually based obligation to provide the spark in relationships. There are spiritual teachings beyond just religious ones that encourage men to be leaders and initiators and women to be receptive and nurtures of that spark. There is some essential truth here in the need for men to stop neutering themselves, to step up, and enjoy their power as they initiate contact, and for women to enjoy it instead of criticizing it for being horny or dominant. This idea can be applied to more than just the beginning of a relationship.

In the area of who initiates sex, for example, I make the same arguments. Both people should initiate it if they want it. I made it clear earlier that relationships work best if desire is shared and balanced somewhat equally. This can be a problem with sexual desire because women are often afraid to initiate sex. But men are afraid to initiate sex, too. We are all afraid of rejection, but men have been trained to initiate anyway. Women's fear may also be because of old norms where women are expected to be passive but also because they don't want to become that which they have judged men for being—too horny or sexual. These fears combined with men's emerging need to be sensitive often results in no one initiating sex.

Another example is when one partner has more need for alone time than the other, yet they deny those needs and remain in close contact when they need time alone. This may cause problems. If they allow themselves to be independent when they need to, they will be able to come back to connection and grow toward becoming increasingly relational (feminine) without suffering the rebellion of having suppressed their instinctual need to be independent.

Remembering that all of these traits are good and important human qualities will help us all grow to be balanced. Perhaps we all need to be more masculine as well as more feminine! If we used our genitalia as metaphors for what I mean here, it would be a good thing if we all acted like (assertive) penises and (receptive) vaginas. If we extended ourselves, reached out, and penetrated and simultaneously received, welcomed and nurtured each other, most of the people I know would be happy. It is important that we not lose our powerful side in the desire to be sensitive.

CHAPTER 42
THE INNER-SEXUAL-SELF

Just as we have an inner-child, a pusher, or a pleaser, we also have inner-sexual-selves. Giving our inner-sexual-self a name can help us to use its energy more consciously and beneficially. I have had clients describe many sexual selves with their own unique descriptions. Some of these have included a lover, a seducer, an inner teenage sexual self, a horny self, a passionate sexual self, a sensuous sexual self, a nurturing sexual self, and so on. It is helpful to embrace the validity of various sexual parts and heal the sexual shame that goes with the suppression of these parts.

The term inner-sexual-self is a general way to address our sexual identity from the inside, instead of from the outside or from how others view us. This gives us an additional way to identify and meet our own needs. To identify our inner-sexual-self, or selves, helps us nurture and self-soothe our needs in much the same way as identifying our inner-child does.

This is a subtle but important distinction. The inner-sexual-self is another way for us to feel our sexual vitality more fully. When we experience our sexual nature on our own, as a quality that is independent of a lover, we claim and hold more power and aliveness within all areas of our life because we are not just limiting our sexual identity to the more specific area of intimate relationship. Our sexual vitality is something we have and cannot lose when a relationship changes form. This also suggests that we add a transpersonal component to our sexual nature. Love and even erotic love is something we can feel transpersonally, meaning beyond our personal relationships with people. Transpersonal love helps us transcend the possessive archetypes and feel love more unconditionally. We can feel an ecstatic sensual connection to life, the earth, and even to friends who are not lovers.

It is my hope that this entire book has helped you contact many inner-sexual-selves, or at least increased your general sense of yourself as a sexual being. Here, I am simply suggesting that you remember to give this energy a name. Having a name will help you hold it within yourself and know that it is an important part of you. Just as a major thesis of this book is that by releasing sexual suppression, we will have more vitality and aliveness available for all forms of intimacy, when we are more connected to our inner sexual selves we can better embrace our entire sexual nature.

❦ PART V ❧
ADDITIONAL RESOURCES

CHAPTER 43
VOICE DIALOGUE AND EMBRACING DISOWNED SELVES

I already covered embracing disowned selves within ourselves and our relationships in Part III of this book, and gave suggestions on how to embrace disowned energies. Aspects of ourselves that we have disowned result in a variety of personal and relationship issues. If we disown something, we limit our ability to manifest or enjoy all aspects of life. Our partner will possess energies that are opposite of ours or disowned, and this becomes part of how we may become reactive to them. Also, disowned energies become a source of attraction or affairs. Eventually we will have attractions to things we have suppressed within us or our relationship.

We all have a monogamous side or monogamous selves as well as a non-monogamous side/selves. Perhaps the simplest summary of this book would be to say that the key to maintaining monogamy is to be aware of both sides of the issue and to make a conscious choice that serves us.

In this chapter, I want to elaborate on the Voice Dialogue technique and how it assists in personal growth. Voice dialogue involves talking to each individual self or sub-personality and learning about its role in our life. As a result, we become more aware of our selves instead of being unconsciously driven by them. This gives us the ability to make choices more consciously.

Choice is a big and complex issue. If choice were easy to execute, personal growth books would be shorter. Notice throughout this book how many different issues of which I have encouraged us to be aware. In addition to the fact that this is a complex topic, one reason for exploring so many details is that by increasing our awareness, we become more deeply in contact with what the issues are, and thus more able to choose upon which aspect of ourselves we want to act. But awareness is not all that is necessary for choice to occur. The more we are aware of, and the closer that brings us to deeper feeling, the closer we come to being able to make new choices. Choice is actually more related to feeling than it is to awareness. Awareness is the first step, but the bigger and more ambiguous step is acceptance, which involves feeling and being in contact with our options on a feeling level. In a "psychology-of-selves" model, it would mean being in full contact with the selves involved on both sides of an issue.

Choice occurs most easily when we no longer have an energetic attachment to an issue. The more we energetically separate from an issue, the freer we are to act in any direction. Here, the phrase "between the opposites lies the path" means the more feeling and awareness we have of each issue, the better. When we feel each opposing issue and understand its energy, the more we will gain the freedom to actually choose one over the other.

There is much involved in this kind of energetic separation, including:

Unraveling the feelings associated with the development of the energy or self. For example, if someone has loss issues and a vulnerable child who fears abandonment, they would likely also develop selves that protect them from the pain of loss by avoiding intimacy or commitment. Resolving this is not as simple as just seeing the selves that are protecting them by avoiding intimacy and choosing to be intimate. To choose new behaviors, they would need to work with their vulnerable child's original feelings of loss, which led to the development of the protection selves, and also work with the protection selves' feelings about intimacy.

Embracing the purpose of these selves: This means listening to each self and understanding how they have each helped to solve problems. It will include embracing their good purpose and how they were protection mechanisms that helped us remain safe and secure. When we talk to a primary self that is non-committal and afraid of intimacy or commitment, we usually discover that its purpose was to keep us safe by keeping us away from the potential loss that can occur if we entered into intimacy or commitment. Our non-committal self's purpose would likely be to help us create greater control or protection and avoid old vulnerabilities.

If we use the opposite example of someone with a strong primary self who chases love and seeks intimacy and commitment, we will likely discover that its purpose is also to create control and protection. The purpose of a chaser self is to create security and protection by going out into the world to procure love.

In either of these examples, the individual would also need to understand and embrace how these primary ways of being are fueled by vulnerable selves or the inner-child underneath them. The purpose of these kinds of stronger primary selves is to protect the vulnerable child.

Connecting with the essence of the self: This means that the more we can be with and embrace the selves' energy and come to know them, the less habitual the selves will be. If we talk to our non-committal self or our chasing self, we connect more directly to its essence. This enables us to separate from it because we can feel its identity as independent from us. By acknowledging its identity, we begin to experience it as having some separation from us.

Energetic separation involves knowing our selves and their purpose, as well as understanding the vulnerable feelings that the selves have helped protect or resolve. This understanding gives us greater contact with their essence and the ability to separate from them when we choose. A key is to feel both the vulnerable feelings and the power or protection issues. Seeing the opposites widens our path.

Voice Dialogue is a therapy or communication tool that has deeply taught me this aspect of the psychology of selves. I use it for myself and with my clients because it enables people to gain an energetic shift that allows for true choice to occur. Working with one self at a time helps people to make conscious choices as to whether or not they want to act on a given self's desire.

Voice Dialogue sessions involve conversing with one self at a time with the help of a trained facilitator. First, the facilitator and client discuss issues from the perspective of which selves are at play in the clients' life and decide which self to talk to first. Then the client physically moves to a place in the room where the self to be dialogued with would most likely be. By moving physically, the self is given its own space. This supports the overall purpose, which is to validate each self's identity, role, and good purpose in the client's life. The facilitator talks to the self without judgment from a position of curiosity.

By giving the client and the self a chance to feel the self's own valuable identity, they are better able to feel and see the difference between the self and their identity as a whole person. This independent awareness creates a separation between the client's overall identity and the self. It is by becoming aware of the self independently and gaining separation from it that the client can use it more consciously. When we identify with selves as though we are the self, their role is habitual. When we realize that they are *parts* of us, we can begin to use them consciously when we feel that they will be helpful.

Voice dialogue facilitators often refer to this process as learning to develop an "Aware Ego." The aware ego can be described as an aware chooser. It is not a self; it is a description of a healthy ego function. This suggests that as we separate from the partial identities of selves, we develop an identity that can operate from a more purely aware place of choice. Often when we first hear this, we think of our observer self or another self, such as our psychological self, which has a great overview of our life. These would not be the aware ego either. While we have selves that have great insight, guidance, and awareness, they are still selves that have roles, identities, and agendas. Once we try to describe the aware ego, we are probably not there. If we are in an aware ego state and we notice it, we have probably left it and are in a self, which is trying to describe the aware ego. In my training with Hal and Sidra Stone, Sidra described it as follows: "The aware ego is like the conductor of the orchestra and the selves are the musicians playing instruments. The aware ego is like a juggler and the selves are the balls or flaming torches being juggled. The aware ego is the driver of the car and the selves are the passengers."

Precisely defining the aware ego is actually not very important. Knowing that it exists *is* important to make it clear that the work is not about getting a perfect set of selves to cooperate with our desires and goals. The key is to separate from all the selves and develop an aware ego. This choice function is a key in life. Optimally, choice is not made from a set of selves. True choice is made by the conductor, juggler, or driver.

Voice dialogue sessions basically involve working with the various pulls or drives in your life. You and your facilitator would usually talk to the selves on both sides of an issue. If you felt you were working too much, you might have a pusher self that is driving you to work. By dialoguing with the pusher self and the selves opposite it who want to play and rest, you can gain the freedom to choose either. If you had the desire to have an affair, you would want to hear from your sexual selves or other non-monogamous selves, as well as your loyal or monogamous selves. You would also benefit from listening to your vulnerable inner-child and see how its needs may be driving the other selves. By connecting with all sides of the issue, you gain greater ability to make a conscious choice. If you are in an abusive or dead relationship, you could gain the strength to leave by working with the selves that felt it was not okay or safe to leave and the selves that wanted to leave.

Couples have an added dimension where each person can learn about how their selves react and respond to their partner's selves. Relationships are complex systems. When two people's issues are interfacing, it results in a multitude of variables. If we simplified ourselves and said we have ten issues or selves involved in our life, and we viewed our success in life based on getting these selves to cooperate with our overall direction, this is complicated enough. But if we add a partner, and see them as bringing another ten issues into the picture, we do not have twenty issues. Together we have ten issues relating to ten issues, which is ten times ten, or one hundred. I don't intend to be discouraging and say that we need to work through one hundred issues in order to achieve our desired results, but relationships are complex. How we react to our partner's issues is the key. If we work on our main reactions, we will find success.

Using the voice dialogue process with couples helps each person clearly see which selves of theirs are reacting to which selves of their partner. This is done by dialoguing with one person's selves at a time and then asking the other partner what they felt as they listened and observed. This provides specific and deep awareness of how our partner triggers us, and how we respond.

An example of this might be that if I talk to one person's pusher and discuss the issues of them working a lot, the partner who is observing is more able to see how they react to this. After the facilitation of the pusher, I would ask the partner who was observing how they react to their partner's pusher. If they said, "I get hurt and then I withdraw," we would then work with them and the self that withdraws, perhaps a hermit self. After working with their hermit self, I would then ask the other how they react to their partner's hermit. If they said, "I get hurt and then I withdraw and work more," we could then work with their withdrawn self, and so on.

At some point, we would also speak directly to the hurt by talking to each person's vulnerable inner-child, which helps the couple let go of defensiveness and reactivity. People don't get defensive in response to the vulnerable inner-child; they get defensive in response to the outer layers that are protecting the child by being critical or withdrawn.

Most good couples' counseling seeks to resolve similar patterns of how defensiveness or reactivity escalates in relationships. I have a saying that I used long before I was trained in voice dialogue, which is "don't react to my reactions." This is a humorous way to indicate that we all inevitably have reactions, to which we hypocritically don't want our partner to react. It is inevitable that reactions will escalate, but a key to success is the couple's ability to interrupt and de-escalate their reactivity. Working with the various selves gives a very clear picture of the reactions. It gives an energetic separation that increases our aware ego and our ability to choose new behaviors, or in this case choose a different reaction.

Reacting to each other is not bad; it is inevitable. The key is to work out the reactions in a healthy manner. I am not suggesting that we become timid or suppressed or resort to hostile confrontation; however, it is important that we learn to address what is really going on in relationships. We are all very sensitive and prone to feeling defensive when we feel criticized. We need to overcome this and learn to address conflict. Voice dialogue gives us a way to be direct about specific issues without attributing the problem to the whole person or giving a sense of condemnation to them as a whole person.

Voice Dialogue also helps us resolve attractions and

evolve relationship patterns, preferences, and arousal patterns. By embracing our disowned energies, we become less attracted to them because we discover them within ourselves. By connecting with all aspects of ourselves, we in essence become everything and are less likely to be pulled in any one direction. By being in touch with all sides of ourselves, we become freer to choose consciously what serves us. For couples, this helps resolve attractions. For singles who seek to attract a partner who is different from their old patterns, voice dialogue enables them to embrace and develop the disowned qualities that prior partners represented, thus enabling them to attract and be attracted to people with whom they have more in common. By embracing the extremes within ourselves, we can consciously choose relationships that fit our central needs. Voice Dialogue is my favorite way of helping myself and others do this.

CHAPTER 44
BREATHWORK AND RESOLVING OUR BIRTH SCRIPT

Breathwork is the most powerful, empowering, spiritual, and effective process I have discovered. It has been central to my understanding of life and relationships and to my development. Breathwork is a process that involves breathing in a full, free manner (as guided by a trained facilitator), which results in an increase in the level of physical and spiritual energy in the body, thus cleansing the many tensions held there. The result of the physical cleansing is that the mental and emotional origins of tension come back into consciousness where they can then be healed. By learning to breathe consciously and fully, we discover and release the core issues now held in our mind and emotions.

It was first named Rebirthing in the early '70s by Leonard Orr, when he and his first clients relived their births and discovered the tremendous impact birth had had upon them. Breathwork has since undergone many changes to become a more holistic process, addressing our entire childhood and life experience. Some breathworkers have not changed the name because understanding the birth experience is one of the valuable results of the process.

Important: As stated earlier, Rebirthing/Breathwork is always about breathing fully and freely and never involves pushing a client through a tunnel of blankets and pillows to reenact birth. The term rebirthing was used in error by therapists to describe a completely different process that involved trying to re-create the birth canal, and these therapists killed an eleven-year-old girl in 2001. Outside of these therapists, and this isolated tragedy, rebirthing is always breathwork that occurs in open air, or occasionally in water, without restriction.

Breathwork's contributions to psychology and personal growth include helping us to understand the effects our birth has had on individual self-esteem, relationships, and family dynamics, as well as specific issues, such as the addictive process and abuse. For most of us, our birth was an early experience of a system where our needs and our mother's needs were often of least importance, and the doctor's needs were most important. For many people, birth was a traumatic event where they felt mistreated.

There are also a wide variety of family issues that affect our birth, such as being unplanned or unwanted, being wanted for the wrong reasons, or our family having a sexual preference. Our childhood was not our first experience of invalidation and is not the only experience from which we're recovering. Breathwork is also of tremendous value to couples that do not want to act out their own birth scripts with their children.

Breathworkers assist their clients by using a wide variety of counseling tools and perspectives. Clients may remember their birth and other early experiences through the breathing process, or with a general discussion of feelings and family knowledge that helps to get a picture of what occurred at the time of their birth. Most breathworkers have a background in nontraditional approaches to healing, as well as respect for some of the more traditional ideas and tools.

A key to all personal healing is to learn to feel again. As a result of early life being too traumatic or intense for us to stay "present," we learned to numb ourselves to avoid feelings. This is the core issue of addiction: some of us use substances and behaviors to accomplish this numbness; others use behaviors. It is my feeling that virtually all of us have this issue. I call it all addiction—the habit of not feeling or not being present. This is a slightly broader definition of addiction than you may be used to, but the inability to feel and be present is an addiction or habit that we don't know how to change and subconsciously think we need in order to survive. Our culture has supported this greatly by suggesting that the source of happiness is outside of us, in things. The subconscious communication is that these things would "fix" our pain. We don't need to be drug-addicted to avoid feeling in a materialistic and sexualized society. Earlier, I discussed the many ways we tend to avoid feeling and not be present with ourselves.

Breathwork gives tremendous support in learning to feel and be present. After doing the process for a while, breathing becomes a moment-by-moment ritual for feeling, healing, and disengaging the need to control. It offers tremendous psychological growth in all areas, including intimate relationships, our relationship with ourselves, and our sexuality, by providing a nonverbal way to heal, which takes most people way beyond more verbal and cognitive therapies. It also results in such powerful emotional and spiritual releases that it addresses one's whole process, from releasing traumas to accepting our self-worth.

Breathwork sessions are generally two hours in length and include counseling in addition to the breathing process. The breathing process usually takes between one and one-and-a-half hours. The experience during the breathing portion varies from session to session, and from client to client. The most basic experience is usually described as a tingling or vibrating sensation. Breathworkers refer to this as an energy release, a cellular cleansing of tension stored in the body. This is a result of the breathing process increasing the level of physical and spiritual energy in the body, which washes away old tensions. This can feel like a subtle and peaceful cleansing, or it can be powerful and specific as tensions are released and mental and emotional issues resurface.

Breathwork begins by working with the physical body to cleanse the emotional and spiritual bodies. This almost always leaves the client in a state somewhere between peace and ecstasy. As simple as it sounds, most clients usually describe it as one of the most amazing experiences they have ever had. It connects you to yourself, your worth, and to your source.

In my practice, I recommend weekly sessions for the first ten to twenty sessions. After about ten sessions, most people can get value from breathwork themselves, and could start to see their facilitator less often. I also recommend people train to become a breathworker at any point. It enhances their personal process and assists them in learning more about breathwork for the purpose of doing the process on their own or trading sessions with other trainees.

CHAPTER 45
HOW TO USE AFFIRMATIONS

An affirmation is a conscious thought that we choose to immerse into our subconscious mind in order to produce a desired result. When working with any psycho-spiritual issue, it helps to discover the operating beliefs and use affirmations to assist us in resolving the issue and changing the behaviors associated with it.

The best affirmations are ones that address our core psychological issues and belief systems. The main affirmations I recommend are the eternal laws—the ones that address our core beliefs and birth scripts. I have never recommended affirmations like, *"I am now manifesting a pink Cadillac"* because they are superficial and fantasy based. It is better to use affirmations that help to resolve feelings of shame or unworthiness. If we feel worthy, manifesting love and money become natural extensions of that state. If our main affirmation was *"I am good enough as a man/woman,"* getting clear on that is what is needed to manifest a pink Cadillac or a monogamous relationship. If we feel good enough, abundance more naturally follows. We could do the affirmations, *"I am good enough as a man/woman to deserve a pink Cadillac"* or *"I am good enough as a man/woman to deserve a monogamous relationship,"* but they are not necessary because the key is to feel good enough. Similarly, if we just did the affirmation, *"I deserve monogamy,"* it is not addressing the underlying issue.

There are many ways to use affirmations. We can write them, record them on tape (endless loop tapes are best) to be listened to, and write them on cards and place them around the house or in our car. Ultimately, the goal is to bring to the surface and resolve old feelings and issues and replace them with the positive thoughts. This is a complex process, which includes virtually every good therapeutic ideal, such as allowing ourselves to feel and unravel the old issues from our emotional bodies. Changing a belief is not just about changing thinking, it is about working with the emotional body to feel and let go of energetic attachment to the old issues. Affirmations are just one tool that can help that process. It is important that they be used in conjunction with working with the associated feelings and emotions.

I have taught affirmations since 1978, and I always point out this emotional body connection by suggesting that we would be better off to scream affirmations than to write them. We need to use them in a way that addresses our core feelings.

As long as we keep in mind that this is an emotional process, writing or taping affirmations, or placing them on cards, can be helpful. The basic technique for writing them is to write them repeatedly (as many as seventy times per day) in all three persons, using our native language and childhood names or nicknames, and include a response column.

Using all three persons means that in addition to saying, *"I, Peter, am good enough,"* I would also say, *"Peter, you are good enough"* and *"Peter is good enough."* If the affirmation is more complex, think of how a friend would say it to you, or how you could say it to another, and you will be able to decide where to place the you or the she/he. Writing in all three persons is important because the negatives get imprinted in all three ways. The conclusions we draw for ourselves are more easily resolved by using the first person or "I." The conclusions we get from others (i.e., if you've been told "you are lazy") are more directly addressed in the second person or "you." The conclusions we get from people talking about us in our presence are more easily addressed in the third person "she/he." Even positive things our parents may have said, like "she/he is so smart" tend to create problems of pressure and perfectionism, which can be addressed with affirmations in the third person.

Using childhood language and names is important because they carry our earliest imprints and will be the easiest way to trigger and release the issues. I have had clients who spoke a different language the first few years of their lives, and can't even speak that language anymore, get value from working with translated affirmations.

The response column means that whatever affirmation technique is used, it is important to notice and feel the negative responses. In writing affirmations, it means actually drawing a vertical line to create a column on the right side of the page. Then as we write affirmations, we can record our responses. This gives us a way to process the old feelings and release them, then return to the affirmation. New insights can be discovered with this process. For example, if I was doing the affirmation, *"I am good enough"* and had a response that was, "No you aren't; you are too big" I could then add the affirmation, *"I am the perfect size"* to my process.

It is a good idea to receive guidance from a facilitator with affirmations. A good facilitator can help you get clear on what the core issues are and turn them into affirmations that truly address them. And remember, affirmations are not a panacea; they are just one way to guide and focus a complex and emotional process.

CHAPTER 46
BREATHWORK AND DISSOLVING BLOCKAGES

Breathwork is the most powerful tool I have discovered for opening up energy, addressing issues at their core, and dissolving blockages to the natural life force in the body. Although breathwork is not a sexual process, it supports spiritual and powerful sexual development by opening up the flow of energy in our body. Since breathwork assists us in dissolving blockages, it helps address sexual issues. Since it opens us up, it makes us more accessible to intimacy. Being open to intimacy is not something we can just do on command. Our issues that make us resist intimacy take a physical form in our body. To be fully opened, we need to resolve barriers and build a body and a psyche that is truly opened on an energetic level. I use the phrase "intimacy threshold" to describe how our psychological openness and clarity dictates how much intimacy we can allow, create, or tolerate. As we grow psycho-spiritually, we increase and expand our intimacy threshold. Our old issues result in blockages in our body, and these blockages inhibit our sexual function.

Breathwork is about all areas of personal growth. It is powerful energy medicine, and it helps to address a wide variety of issues at their core. By opening us up and clearing issues in our energy field, it helps us grow and evolve sexually, just as it helps us grow as parents, friends, teachers, psychics, and humans.

CHAPTER 47
SACRED SEXUALITY

Sacred sexuality is a term that many teachers use to describe philosophies and practices that encourage us to view sex as a sacred spiritual experience. Many of these ideas originated from the Hindu practice of Tantra. Tantra is a spiritual practice that includes some sexual aspects but is about more than just sex. As Tantra has been taught in the west, the emphasis has been primarily on the sexual aspect, so that is what is most often noted. There are many aspects to the sexual components of Tantra or Sacred Sexuality, but my simplified definition is "the art and science of using sexual energy to increase spiritual and emotional energy and connection." Even this definition is somewhat silly because in an ideal world, I should not have to note that sexual energy is part of our spiritual and emotional energy. Ideally, we would all have grown up knowing that good sex is not just physical, and that it supports our spiritual, emotional, and physical beings.

Many spiritual belief systems or practices view our life force as originating from our feet or the base of our spine and flowing up our body. Whether we call this energy prana, kundalini, chi, or just our life force, there is a consensus among many philosophies and holistic approaches that the more open we are physically, emotionally, and spiritually, the more this life energy flows freely up our body and the healthier we are as a result. Various models address this in their own way. For example in Chinese medicine, our life force travels along energy meridians. A purpose of acupuncture is to keep these meridians opened. Central to the Hindu or tantric model is the idea of chakras, which are energy centers that are within the body. The chakras are located in various areas of the body, and each has a different spiritual or emotional function. Each chakra contains and generates different issues. For example, our love and grief issues are held in our heart chakra.

For my purposes here, I will use the idea of the chakras to illustrate the value of viewing our sexual energy as traveling up our body, thus enabling us to use this energy for our overall development. If we have blocked issues in these energy centers, the blockages will affect our entire life, including our sexuality. This not only inhibits our experience in that area of the body but also to the areas above it. For example, if we have unresolved issues that result in a blockage in our third chakra (our solar plexus), then our sexual or life energy will stop there during lovemaking, and we will not be able to experience the aliveness or sexual intimacy of the chakras above it, one of which is the heart. We will not be able to fully experience the intimacy that goes with a deep heart connection.

Some simple working definitions of each chakra will further explain that a key to full sexual connection is to resolve life issues. What is also inspiring about sacred sexuality is that this practice of using our sexual energy to help us bring energy up our spine helps us dissolve energy blockages and resolve virtually any life issue. I do not claim to have full expertise of the chakras, but these names and ideas will give you enough information to begin to view lovemaking and sex in a whole new way.

At the base of our spine between our genitals and anus is our first, or root, Chakra. This chakra is about our connection to the earth and our connection to our collective society or tribe. Our second chakra is a few inches below our navel and is the chakra of creativity or creative power and sexuality. The third is our power chakra at our solar plexus, below where our ribs join. This is where we hold our identity, freedom, and self-esteem issues. The fourth is our heart chakra and the center of love and unconditional love, both for ourselves and for others. The fifth chakra is our throat chakra and where we express ourselves and our truths. It is also about our will and free choice. The sixth is our third eye, which is between our eyes in our forehead. This is the energy center for perception, vision, and intuition. The seventh is our crown chakra and where we connect to the infinite or to spirit (or God).

Many teachings also talk of additional chakras that exist above the head, which connect us more deeply to the spiritual realms, but I find the first seven to be more relevant to being in relationships and to being emotionally present in the physical body.

When we are sexually aroused, we are increasing the life force that is traveling up our body. If we hit a block in a chakra, the energy stops and our sexual experience becomes limited. For example, if we have sexual shame issues held within our second chakra, the life energy that the sexual energy is accelerating will become blocked. The range of emotion and intimacy of the sexual experience will be limited to the issues of the first and second chakra. Lovemaking would then have the excitement and desire of the first two chakras but would lack the heart and spirituality of the upper chakras.

If we have low self-esteem or identity issues that constrict the flow of energy in or solar plexus or power chakra, then we would not be as able to feel our power in lovemaking. Nor would we be as able to let energy move above it into our heart, voice, perception, and spiritual connection energy centers.

The same is true for any chakra or issue. For example, if we have wounds that we are holding in our heart, we would be less likely to allow the energy of lovemaking into our heart. This gives us an important image: that we can also use the energy of lovemaking to confront the issues we hold in our bodies. Imagine a couple making love and not allowing the energy into their hearts. Imagine them fearing what would happen. It is as if they are making sure that they don't open up, get vulnerable, or burst into tears. Imagine another couple that feels safe enough with each other that they can allow these feelings to come up. Imagine them making love, looking into each other's eyes, and expressing love, joy, and vulnerability. Imagine the energy in their hearts swelling and one or both of them bursting into tears. They might know why they are crying or they might not. They might be filled with a joyous sadness regarding how beautiful the experience of lovemaking is, or they might be aware of an old wound surfacing. It doesn't really matter. Something clear about this image is that they are having a deep and intimate experience.

This image also points out many basic issues, such as

the importance of communication and being comfortable with another person's feelings. For example, I feel that we should not assume that we should stop making love just because our partner is crying. We should ask them if they want to stop or if they are okay, but we should not assume that they are having a negative experience. If our partner is wincing in pain or holding their breath, we should certainly stop and ask them if they are okay. There are many things to be sensitive to, but we do not need to react with our fears and shut down ourselves. People often cry while making love, especially after orgasm. They may or may not be able to articulate what they are feeling. The main thing that they are likely to need is for their partner to stay with them emotionally and physically.

Another simple part of this image is that, as this couple's hearts are opening, it is helpful if they talk about their experience. By putting some voice to the feelings, the energy is moving up through their hearts and into their throat chakra. By opening their voice, they are giving birth to the feeling below in their hearts. Here my model becomes a little less linear and points out that if we can put words to any block, we help that block to open. A major assertion of this model is that if we are blocked in our lower energy centers (which is where our more emotional issues are held), we will limit the energy we allow in our upper energy centers (which is where our more spiritual energy is held). So, by opening up our lower body, we allow the energy to move upward, but we can also use the assets of the upper energy centers, such as communication, to invite the energy up. This is to say that a spiritually opened person can use the strengths they possess in their upper energy centers to help them resolve emotional blocks in their lower energy centers. Working with what is opened in us helps us free any less opened areas.

Imagine a young man who is quite blocked emotionally and in his heart, but in the area of sexual desire is not blocked. He can use his sex drive to expand his energy and address these deeper emotional and spiritual issues. If he doesn't expand his energy, as the sexual desire travels up his body, he will orgasm prematurely. This model of tantra is helpful with premature ejaculation. Premature ejaculation is caused by intense energy that has no path for release except through orgasm. If the individual can open up and allow more energy to travel up their body, they will be able to postpone orgasm. If they do orgasm (if that is their choice), it is also more of a full body orgasm.

There are many details that are taught about tantra. They can include meditative and visual processes for creating connection before making love, techniques for having more stimulating lovemaking, and ideas for having more intimate lovemaking. Personally, I value connection and intimacy. I find that if my partner and I have intimacy, we naturally have more powerful and stimulating sex. I view the practice of tantra as using our sexual experience to open up and learn to have full, intimate connection in our whole being. This not only results in exquisitely deep personal connection with our lover, but it is also healing.

Key Tantric or Sacred Sexuality Tools

First is communication. This includes virtually anything about which a couple would need to talk. It includes everything in this book and more. It means creating good communication habits, learning to speak up about what we feel, and being on a path of increasing our emotional intelligence. Good communication requires that we feel safe with each other both physically and emotionally. This, in turn, increases our feeling safe with one another. Good communication also includes being able to talk about sex and sexual desire and preferences. Good communication is important in our entire life and also while making love. Good communication creates connection, safety, and trust. Communication opens us up to each other. Communication is the ultimate foreplay, and it is occurring all day long.

It is worth noting here that I agree with the popular notion that women often need more communication and non-sexual connection before making love than men do. It has been said that women need connection to feel sexual, and men need sex to feel connected. This has resulted in long lasting power struggles and is part of why there are many celibate partnerships. I hope that this entire book has made it clear that I basically favor the female perspective on this. I find it more workable for men to slow down and learn to be more connected. I don't think it works as well to ask women to hurry up and be sexual.

I like to illustrate this with an example of two people who jog or run together. If one is faster than the other, they will have to run the slower speed if they want to run together. My earlier discussions of desire also speak to this. It is mathematically inevitable that a relationship will be governed by the lower desire. But with communication and connection, nobody really loses anything. Everyone benefits from increased connection, safety, and trust. If men honor the timing and pace women need to be connected before making love, the end result is love and sexual intimacy. It is actually a minor point that the man would be ready for sexual intimacy sooner.

Connection is the ultimate foreplay. Things like cooking, cleaning, and daily conversation, which we might view as non-sexual, are part of the sexual sphere of life. Connection is the real issue. Lovemaking is an ultimate expression of connection. It is not reasonable for us just to dive into a sexual connection if we feel disconnected the rest of the day. It is important to view our whole life and daily activity as part of the connecting process and treat every aspect of life as an expression of our connection. When we consider our partner's needs in every area—kitchen, bathroom, finances, health, scheduling, gardening, children, friends, and more—then they will become better able to connect with us in the bedroom.

Next, I want to mention a couple of things that apply to lovemaking. The key ones are to make love with the lights on, make eye contact most of the time, to breathe, slow down when you want to delay orgasm, and let go of goal-oriented sex (i.e., trying to have foreplay lead to intercourse and intercourse lead to orgasm).

The lights have to be on if you're going to be making eye contact and see each other. Intimacy means, "in-to-me-see." Lovemaking is deeper, more spiritual, and emotional if it is about feeling a deep connection with our partner. This does not mean that there isn't value in just closing our eyes and receiving, or as David Schnarch says, "being done." It just means that the most basic component of sacred sex is about seeing each other.

Breathing is essential for good lovemaking. By breathing and pulling energy up the body into higher chakras, we can experience more frequent or more powerful orgasms.

Breathing is the most basic tool for managing the flow of energy in the body, both for expanding the energy to increase sensation but also for expanding it so it doesn't explode early in the form of a premature orgasm. Slowing down is the other key tool for delaying orgasm. This is most applicable to men and particularly younger men, but it means that if you want to delay orgasm, tell your partner you need to hold still for a minute and while you do, use your breath to pull the energy up your body. This is, in essence, a way to pull the energy up into your upper chakras. Breathwork is the best way I have found for people to learn to do this. While breathwork isn't sexual, it teaches us how to use our breath to move energy. The biggest mistake men make here is thinking that they shouldn't stop because it will interrupt their partner's movement toward orgasm. Another mistake they make is to just be selfish and not want to stop their own orgasm. One basic point of this whole chapter is that many people prefer to make love for a longer intimate period than be driven by the goal of orgasm.

And guess what? When we delay orgasm, it comes back even stronger. Central to this knowledge is that sexual arousal doesn't flow best in a straight line upward toward orgasm; if we were to diagram sexual arousal, we would see that it actually flows best when it goes up, then drops down, then back up, and so on. The ultimate tantra is cooking together and getting aroused and then stopping, then kissing and stopping, then communicating and opening up to each other on a deeper level, then another activity, then some foreplay, then more sexual contact— then, even stopping to put on a condom or insert a diaphragm can be seen as a sacred break. Being together in this flow is the key.

Orgasm is secondary. In fact, in true tantra, both men and women withhold orgasm all together. This gets into a spiritual belief that it is best to hold the energy from orgasm in, and not dissipate it by orgasming. I value the emotional effect of not orgasming, which leaves us with increased love and desire for our partner. The true tantric couple leaves the bedroom and still can't keep their hands off each other. Others prefer what I call tantric orgasm, which means that they use the sexual energy to increase intimacy and healing, delay orgasm, and make love for longer periods of time, but they also like the pleasure of orgasm.

Another key point is that trying to orgasm, or being goal-oriented, leads to performance anxiety and causes other problems. If people can't be in the moment with each aspect of intimacy throughout the day, they will end up resisting intimacy and be less likely to create enough intimacy to want to be sexual. For example, imagine a woman that has some resistance to sexual intimacy. We all have some. If she views kissing as a step toward sex, she will be more likely to resist the kiss. If she just views it as a kiss and enjoys it unconditionally, the kiss will be more likely to lead to more and more intimate acts. If she wants to be more sexual, the best way to do so is for her to stop pressuring herself and to just enjoy each act of love as it occurs and see what happens. She will need support from her partner to do this.

One key to all of this is that they both need to be in the moment with each point of contact and be willing to stop at any point. She has to be willing to kiss, to make out, to fondle and be fondled, and then stop without fear of being criticized.

Clearly our culture has called people teases to try to control their sexual boundaries. We all need free choice if we are going to move forward without resisting or rebelling from others. If we can't stop, we are not free to start. If we are free to start or continue without being made wrong if we stop, we will be more likely to start and continue. This applies all the way to intercourse and orgasm. Both partners need to be free to not want to (or be able to) orgasm. If we are pressuring ourselves to go all the way to orgasm, we are not truly free to enjoy the contact that is there.

This can also be understood if you bring in the notion of perfectionism. A basic issue of perfectionism is that, by feeling that something has to be perfect, we will be less likely to start it. If a child feels pressure about being good at an activity, they will not want to try it. This applies to anything from schoolwork to athletics or art. If they feel the picture has to be perfect, they will not want to begin to draw it. If they feel relaxed and feel that whatever they do will be good enough, they will then be more able to participate. Perfectionism paralyzes us. In lovemaking, perfectionism leads to performance anxiety, and the best way to let go of it is to let go of the idea that foreplay has to lead to intercourse, and intercourse has to lead to orgasm, and so on.

Another example of this is that, if a man is afraid he won't be able to bring a woman to orgasm, his anxiety will have similar effects. He might avoid sex all together. He might get so stressed it leads to premature orgasm. Here it would be as if his unconscious fear of not pleasing the woman would lead to his not trying, so he might just give up, be selfish, and orgasm early. Of course, it is not a man's job to bring a woman to orgasm. Many couples will benefit from just letting go of orgasm all together and explore sexuality without that pressure. If this feels right for you, I would suggest you talk about it and make it an expressed goal for you not to orgasm. A woman could have that goal and the man could still orgasm if he wants. Some men would have to work on their own ego to be able to do this, but it is very important that the man's ego not accentuate the woman's performance anxiety. We are all responsible for our own pleasure and our self-esteem.

This point also applies to how we need to be free to have foreplay without it leading to sex. If we kiss our lover and tie their response to our worth, we leave the moment. We need to kiss them for the kiss's sake and not to turn them on and prove our worth. They need to be having their own kiss for themselves. They are freer to do this if our need to prove our worth is not subconsciously pressuring them.

Sacred sexuality is about love, not sex. It is about having sexual contact be about love and celebration. In this way, every touch is a celebration that is complete within itself.

CHAPTER 48
EPILOGUE

Many parts of me did not want to write this book. I feel that I was spiritually "drafted" or "called" to write it. While my teachings have always included the topic of sexuality, as the decade of the '90s evolved, I became increasingly comfortable sharing about my sexuality and teaching about sexuality in general. As I did this, I found my students and clients very much wanted support in speaking up about their own sexual issues. As I headed in the direction of being willing to discuss sex and sexuality on deeper and deeper levels, the response was very positive. I found myself drafted to head in what was sometimes a scary direction. I often wished that I could just stick to less controversial topics, and I occasionally received criticism.

More importantly, many students thanked me for my direction and my willingness to create a forum for working on sexuality and sexual issues. Somewhere within all of that, I conceived of this book, and the draft continued. I was asked to teach more and more workshops on sexuality and sacred sexuality. Many friends read the manuscript as it evolved and encouraged me to continue to write what they felt was a good and important book.

I have long felt that teaching is not as simple as the adage, "We teach best what we need most." While I find truth in this, I have also always said, "We teach best, what we teach best." As a result of writing this book, I have added the adage, "Be careful what you teach" or more specifically, "Be careful what you want to teach with integrity."

By declaring that I wanted to write this book, I set into motion some very powerful lessons. I ended up dealing with the book's material on a very deep level. I have learned more about unconditional love since I began than I could ever have imagined. I've had deep experiences of what it means to let go of the possessive archetypes and self-soothe. I have learned that unconditional love is beyond human understanding. I am impressed by how deeply intertwined life, love, and sexuality are. I am humbled by how many feelings exist within the arena of personal, sensuous, and sexual love. I have been shown ecstasy and sexual intimacy, and I have been shown the deepest most personal loss I could imagine. I have also experienced the highest highs of celebrating being here as a physical being and being in intimate contact with another.

It took me five years to finish this manuscript, and more years to pursue publishing it. Many times I stopped for months at a time, ostensibly because I lacked the time, only to realize later that I needed more experience, knowledge, feedback, and sensitivity. While I could have articulated almost all of this information many years prior, I needed time to continue my own process so that it could come out of me more clearly and appropriately. I share this book with you in the spirit of discovery. I thank the many friends and clients who have helped me find better and better ways of seeing the information, and better and better voices for delivering the information. I thank spirit for giving me the lessons I needed to shape the book in a direction that would best serve me and the men and women I love. I hope that I have shaped it in a way that serves you.

With Love,
Peter

For more information you can contact me or visit my web sit at www.peterkane.org

SUGGESTED READING LIST

Reading has actually never been the primary vehicle for my learning, but here is a partial list of books I have found helpful in my own work and in my practice. I have divided this list into three general areas.

Breathwork, Pre and Peri-natal Psychology, and Relationship work that was developed by breathworkers:

Begg, Deike. *Freedom from Your Past.* Thorsons, 1999.
Chamberlain, D. *Babies Remember Birth.* St. Martins Press, 1988.
Dowling, Catherine. *Rebirthing and Breathwork.* Judy Piatkus Limited, 2000.
Jones, Eve. *An Introduction to Rebirthing for Health Professionals.* Life Unlimited Books, 1982.
Leboyer, F. *Birth without Violence.* Alfred A. Knopf, Inc., 1975.
Laut, Phil. *Money Is My Friend.* Trinity Press, 1978.
Leonard, Jim & Laut, Phil. *Integrative Rebirthing: the Science of Enjoying All of Your Life.* Trinity Publications, 1983.
Mandel, B. *Open Heart Therapy.* Celestial Arts, 1984.
Manne, Joy. *Soul Therapy.* North Atlantic Books, 1983.
Minett, Gunnel. *Breath and Spirit.* The Aquarian Press, 1994.
Morningstar, Jim. *Spiritual Psychology: A Course for Renewal in Body, Mind and Spirit.* Transformations Incorporated, 1998.
Morningstar, Jim. *Family Awakening, in Body, Mind and Spirit.* Transformations Incorporated, 1984.
Morningstar, Jim. *Breathing in Light and Love, Your Call to Breath and Body Mastery.* Transformations Incorporated, 1994.
Orr, L. & Ray, S. *Rebirthing in the New Age.* Celestial Arts, 1977.

Ray, Sondra. *I Deserve Love*. Celestial Arts, 1976.
Ray, Sondra. *Loving Relationships*. Celestial Arts, 1980.
Ray, Sondra. *Loving Relationships II*. Celestial Arts, 1992.
Ray, Sondra. *Celebration of Breath*. Celestial Arts, 1983.
Ray, S., & Mandel, R. *Birth and Relationships*. Celestial Arts, 1987.
Verny, T., & Kelly, J. *The Secret Life of the Unborn Child*. Summit Books, 1981.
Minett, Gunnel. *Breath and Spirit*. Aquarian/Thorsons, 1994.

The Psychology of Selves and The Voice Dialogue Process:

Dyak, Miriam. *The Voice Dialogue Facilitator's Handbook*. L.I.F.E. Energy Press. 1999.
Stone, H. & Stone, S. *Embracing Ourselves: The Voice Dialogue Manual*. Nantaraj, 1998.
Stone, H. & Stone, S. *Embracing your Inner Critic*. Harper San Francisco, 1993.
Stone, H. & Stone, S. *Embracing Each Other: How to Make All Your Relationships Work for You*. Nantaraj, 1989.
Stone, H. & Stone, S. *Partnering: A New Kind of Relationship*. Nantaraj, 2000.
Stone, S. *The Shadow King: The Invisible Force That Holds Women Back*. Nantaraj, 2000.

Other Books of Interest:

A Course in Miracles. Foundation for Inner Peace, 1975.
Cermak, Timmen. *A Time To Heal: The Road to Recovery for Adult Children of Alcoholics*. Avon Books, 1988.
Coontz, Stephanie. *The Way We Never Were: American Families and the Nostalgia Trap*. BasicBooks, 1992.
Gawain, S. *Creative Visualization*. Whatever Publishing, 1978.
Gibran, Kahlil. *The Prophet*. Wordsworth Editions, 1996.
Hay, Louise. *Heal Your Body*. Hay House Inc., 1982.
Hendrix, Harville. *Getting The Love You Want: A Guide For Couples*. Harper and Row, 1990.
Katie, Byron, & Mitchell, Steven. *Loving What Is: Four Questions That Can Change Your Life*. Three Rivers Press, 2002.

Levine, Steven & Levine, Ondrea. *Embracing the Beloved: Relationship as a Path of Awakening*. First Anchor Books, 1996.

Miller, Alice. *The Drama of the Gifted Child: The Search for the True Self*. Basic Books, 1981.

Moore, Thomas. *The Soul of Sex: Cultivating Life as an Act of Love*. Harper Collins, 1998.

Myss, Caroline. *Anatomy of the Spirit: The Seven Stages of Power and Healing*. Random House, 1997.

Orloff, Judith. *Dr. Judith Orloff's Guide to Intuitive Healing: 5 Steps to Physical, Emotional, and Sexual Wellness*. Random House, 2000.

Orloff, Judith. *Emotional Freedom: Liberate Yourself from Negative Emotions and Transform Your Life*. Random House, 2009.

Pearce, C. Joseph. *Magical Child*, Bantam, 1977.

Ruiz, Don Miguel. *The Four Agreements*. Amber Allen, 1997.

Schaef, Anne. *Escape From Intimacy: Untangling the "Love" Addictions: Sex, Romance, Relationships*. Harper and Row, 1989.

Schnarch, D. *Constructing The Sexual Crucible: An Integration of Sexual and Marital Therapy*. Norton, 1991.

Schnarch, D. *Passionate Marriage: Keeping Love and Intimacy Alive in Emotionally Committed Relationships*. Norton, 1997.

Teutsch, J. & Teutsch, C. *From Here to Greater Happiness*. Price, Stern, Sloan. 1959.

Tolle, Eckhart. *A New Earth: Awakening Your Life's Purpose*. Plume, 2006.

Tolle, Eckhart. *The Power of Now: A Guide To Spiritual Enlightenment*. New World Library, 1999.

Weinhold, Barry. *Playing Grown Up is Serious Business: Breaking Free of Addictive Family Patterns*. Stillpoint Publishing. 1985.

Weinhold, Barry & Weinhold, Janae. *Breaking Free of the Co Dependency Trap*. Stillpoint Publishing, 1989.

Weiss, L. & Weiss, J. *Recovery from Co-Dependency: It's Never Too Late To Reclaim Your Childhood*. Health Communications Inc., 1989.

Welwood, John. *Love and Awakening: Discovering the Sacred Path of Intimate Relationship*. Harper Collins, 1997.

Williamson, Marianne. *Enchanted Love: The Mystical Power of Intimate Relationships*. Simon and Schuster, 1999.

Zukav, Gary. *The Seat of the Soul*. Fireside, 1990.

Breinigsville, PA USA
21 February 2011
256050BV00003B/3/P